Introducing Trevarthen

Colwyn Trevarthen's seminal work has earned him a place alongside the most prestigious thinkers, writers and researchers into human development. He is universally acknowledged as the pre-eminent expert on foetal, neonatal and early childhood development. Sandra Smidt examines the impact of his scientific training, linked to his interest in how filmed episodes of mother or father/baby interactions might inform his understanding about early sociocultural development, encouraging us to view the human infant with fresh eyes and realise how purposive human behaviour is from the start. His interest in and collaborations with others introduce the reader to the idea of communicative musicality, which, together with physical movement, lead the child to acquiring language. This book focuses on the earliest years of life and makes complex ideas accessible and applicable to a range of settings.

As well as providing a glossary of key terms and an introduction to the life and work of Trevarthen, the book is split into three parts: *From foetus to neonate*, *The remainder of the first year of life* and *From one to three*. Each part offers case studies, practical examples, draws on recent research evidence and includes helpful pointers for students labelled 'Think about this'. This essential guide to his work will be of interest to professionals working with children in early childhood settings and to undergraduate students training to become early childhood professionals.

Sandra Smidt is a writer and consultant in early years education. Her publications include *Multilingualism in the Early Years*, *Introducing Bruner*, *Introducing Vygotsky* and *The Developing Child*.

Introducing Early Years Thinkers
Series editor: Sandra Smidt

For more information about this series please visit: www.routledge.com/
Introducing-Early-Years-Thinkers/book-series/IEYT

Introducing Bronfenbrenner
Hayes, O'Toole and Halpenny

Introducing Bruner
Smidt

Introducing Freire
Smidt

Introducing Malaguzzi
Smidt

Introducing Piaget
Halpenny and Pettersen

Introducing Trevarthen
Smidt

Introducing Vygotsky
Smidt

Introducing Trevarthen

A Guide for Practitioners and Students in Early Years Education

Sandra Smidt

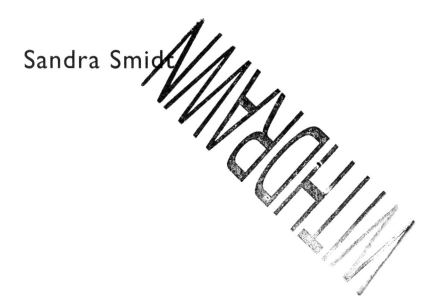

 Routledge
Taylor & Francis Group

LONDON AND NEW YORK

First published 2018
by Routledge
2 Park Square, Milton Park, Abingdon, Oxon OX14 4RN

and by Routledge
711 Third Avenue, New York, NY 10017

Routledge is an imprint of the Taylor & Francis Group, an informa business

British Library Cataloguing in Publication Data
A catalogue record for this book is available from the British Library

Library of Congress Cataloging in Publication Data
Names: Smidt, Sandra, 1943- author.
Title: Introducing Trevarthen : a guide for practitioners and students
in early years education / Sandra Smidt.
Description: Abingdon, Oxon ; New York, NY : Routledge, 2018. |
Series: Introducing early years thinkers
Identifiers: LCCN 2017015287| ISBN 9781138221048 (hardback) |
ISBN 9781138221055 (pbk.) | ISBN 9781315411293 (ebook)
Subjects: LCSH: Early childhood education--Psychological aspects. |
Developmental psychology. | Trevarthen, Colwyn.
Classification: LCC LB1139.23 .S645 2018 | DDC 372.21--dc23
LC record available at https://lccn.loc.gov/2017015287

ISBN: 978-1-138-22104-8 (hbk)
ISBN: 978-1-138-22105-5 (pbk)
ISBN: 978-1-315-41129-3 (ebk)

Typeset in Bembo
by Saxon Graphics Ltd, Derby
Printed and bound by CPI Group (UK) Ltd, Croydon, CR0 4YY

Contents

Preface

In writing this book I have had many interesting and relevant informal discussions and interactions with and from members of my family and my friends. Hazel Abel shared with me episodes in the development of her grandson, born as I started writing this book and now having already had his first birthday as the book faces publication. Jonathan Miller – who knows more about communication and gesture than anyone else I know, talked to me about what he had been reading and introduced me to the work of Susan Goldin-Meadow. And my thanks go to Jess Buckle, David Mindel, Stella Mindel and Hannah Gardiner for permission to use the photographs in this book. Also, of course to Colwyn himself who read the book and made detailed suggestions in his careful and critical reading of it.

Almost a year ago I decided to approach Colwyn Trevarthen, Emeritus Professor at the University of Edinburgh to ask if he would agree to me writing a book about his work. When I told him that the book would become the seventh in a series of books about great thinkers in the field of early childhood – including Lev Vygotsky and Jerome Bruner – he said he would be honoured to be in such august company. So I duly made my way to Edinburgh to spend a day with him. This book is the first one in this series to be dedicated specifically to the development of babies and toddlers. It is in this arena that his work has become known throughout the world. It tells us the story of how the human infant makes herself part of her family, community and culture through her intentional interactions with others. Trevarthen is primarily an evolutionary biologist and neuropsychologist, a philosopher and scientist, and his written work is scholastic and academic. Film plays an important part in his life and work and the illustrative use of film clips in his presentations and online reveals him as a warm and approachable man with a sense of humour, a passionate interest in babies and toddlers and a whimsical way of creating titles for his published papers. Trevarthen, unlike the thinkers discussed in other books in the *Introducing Early Years Thinkers* series – like Piaget, Vygotsky, Bruner and others – says that he is not particularly interested in cognition but rather in conation. If you don't know what that means don't worry: the language he uses in his academic writing is often very specialised and for that reason you will find a glossary of unfamiliar words after this Preface. Conation, as you will see, means having to do with intentions. Trevarthen is more interested in what human infants purposefully do in order to be part of the worlds of others than in how they are learning facts. He also says that he loses interest in babies once they start to speak because then they become like everyone else, a talker who shares, and argues about, conventional ideas! So this book will be different from the others in the series in the following small ways:

- It is written for those involved with babies and toddlers who automatically include those caring for and interacting with them in and away from the home – parents, grandparents, carers, practitioners, teachers and early years professionals.
- It invites you, the reader, to sometimes access Trevarthen's work online following a link or using your browser. There you can find brief film clips he uses to illustrate the points he is making or listen to and see his online presentations. I really recommend that you do this because it brings his work to life. Some of these are on YouTube.
- It is the only book in the series to have been written about someone who is still alive and contributing to our knowledge.
- Every so often throughout the book you will come across sections called *Think about this*, where you will find some issues or examples that ask you to think carefully and come to your own conclusion about what is being said. They invite you to interact with the text.
- In the text where you see a word or phrase underlined it means you can find its meaning by going to the 'New Vocabulary' glossary section.

Note: As in all my books I will refer to her rather than him when citing a generic child. I will also use the convention of usually talking about mother as the primary caregiver although I am well aware that fathers and others can also be primary caregivers and that they bring other sorts of wisdom and creativity to their life with the young person.

The layout of the book

The focus of this book is tracking the human infant from gestation to the age of about three. The book is divided into sections with several chapters in each section. The sections are progressive but it is important to state that the ages cited are merely suggestions: some babies will be doing things sooner or later than others.

A new vocabulary

A glossary of new or unfamiliar/ specialist words

The words in the text that are underlined are defined here. Do use this glossary when you encounter new or unfamiliar words.

adaptations: In biological terms this means the process of change by which an organism or species becomes better suited to active use of its environment.

affect attunement: Attunement is what happens during an interaction between mother and child, where they match their responses and feelings to one another. This is my definition. There are other ways of interpreting this.

affective interaction: A term drawn from psychology to describe the interrelationships between family members.

affective neuroscience: Brain science examining the self-regulation and motivating systems of the brains of all mammals, which retain control of feelings and their sharing in human consciousness and the development of cultural understanding however this is communicated. It is a field developed by the work of the neuroscientist and psychologist Jaak Panksepp.

analogic: It means in comparison with.

anoetic: A state of mind consisting of pure sensation or emotion without cognitive content.

attachment bond: An emotional bond between an infant or toddler and primary caregiver, a strong bond being vital for the child's normal behavioural and social development. An enduring emotional bond that develops between one adult and another in an intimate relationship; romantic attachment.

attention: Can mean the act of close or careful observing or listening; or the power to keep the mind on something; the ability to concentrate.

attunement: Attunement and attachment are related. Attachment is an emotional bond to another person. According to psychologist John Bowlby, the earliest bonds formed by children with their parents (caregivers) have an important impact that continues throughout their life.

Attunement and attachment are related in that mothers/fathers (caregivers) who are available and attuned to their child, in other words, responsive to their child's needs beginning in infancy, establish a sense of security within that child. The infant/child learns that their parent (caregiver) is dependable. This attunement creates a strong foundation for which that child can explore the world. I love the fact that Trevarthen uses the term to describe communicative musicality: tunes in music?

bands (as used by Gray): Small, intimate, trusting groups of people.

behavioural matching: The infant's attempt to copy or mimic the behaviour of adults.

behavioural mimicry: Behavioural mimicry occurs when a person unwittingly imitates the behaviours of another person.

bimanual: Using both hands.

binocular stereopsis: The dictionary defines this as being able to see depth in a three-dimensional world using the information given by both eyes of an individual with normally developed binocular vision.

biobehavioural: The dictionary defines this as of, relating to or involving the interaction of behaviour and biological processes.

cadence: Related to music, this is defined as modulation or inflection of the voice. It is synonymous with tempo, metre, measure, rise and fall, beat, pulse, rhythmical flow/pattern, swing, lilt, cadency. It can be used with regard to speech as in 'there is a biblical cadence in the last words he utters'. For Trevarthen it often refers to the coda – a sequence of notes or chords comprising the close of a musical phrase: 'the final cadences of the Prelude'.

cell differentiation: Cell differentiation is how generic embryonic cells become specialised cells. This occurs through a process called gene expression. Gene expression is the specific combination of genes that are turned on or off (expressed or repressed), and this is what dictates how a cell functions.

circadian rhythms: A daily rhythmic activity cycle based on 24-hour intervals, which is exhibited by many organisms.

climax: The most intense, exciting or important point of something; the culmination.

coactive: Can mean compulsory or restrictive but also acting together.

coda: An ending part of a piece of music or a work of literature or drama that is separate from the earlier parts.

coherence-producing linguistic devices: This is a linguistic term concerned with how there are different ways of making language make sense.

collaborative learning: Learning with others.

communicative musicality: Malloch and Trevarthen define musicality as the expression of our human desire for cultural learning, our innate skill for moving, remembering and planning in sympathy with others that makes our appreciation and production of an endless variety of dramatic temporal narratives possible – whether those narratives consist of specific cultural forms of music, dance, poetry or ceremony; whether they are the universal narratives of a mother and her baby quietly conversing with one another; whether it is the wordless emotional and motivational narrative that sits beneath a conversation between two or more adults or between a teacher and a class.

conation: This is difficult to explain. It is said to be a natural tendency to make an effort to act on feelings and thoughts. So the conative part of the brain drives how one does this.

contingent: It means dependent on, occurring or existing only if something …

contingent effects: There are seven meanings: likely but not certain to happen; possible but not logically necessary; happening by chance or unforeseen causes; subject to chance or unseen effects; unpredictable; intended for use in circumstances not completely foreseen; dependent on or conditioned by something else determined by free choice.

corpus callosum: A broad band of nerve fibres joining the two hemispheres of the brain.

cranial nerves: Nerves that emerge from or enter the skull (or cranium) as opposed to spinal nerves, which come from the vertebral column.

cultural tools: The key to human intelligence or what makes us different from the animals is the ability to make and use tools to extend not only our physical abilities but also our cognitive abilities. So cultural tools are the symbolic systems we use to communicate, express and analyse reality. They may include signs, symbols, maps, plans, numbers, musical notation, pictures, models and, above all, spoken language.

dispositions: This means habits of minds. They can be positive or negative.

dyad: A dyad is a pair. In Trevarthen's work it mostly refers to an infant and mother or other primary caregiver.

dyadic: An interaction between two people.

ecology: The branch of biology that deals with the relations of organisms to one another and their physical surroundings

egalitarian: This means fairly distributed or equal.

emotional envelope: A safe space between the mother or other caregiver and baby.

empathy: The ability to share the feelings of another.

encode: Convert into a coded form or when thinking of biochemistry for a gene to be responsible for producing a substance or behaviour.

environment of evolutionary adaptedness (EEA): The environment of evolutionary adaptedness (EEA) refers to the environment in which a given adaption is said to have evolved. The term was coined by John Bowlby as part of his attachment theory.

epigenetic: Epigenetics literally means 'above' or 'on top of' genetics and refers to external modifications to DNA that turn genes 'on' or 'off'. These modifications do not change the DNA sequence, but instead, they affect how cells 'read' genes.

ethology: The science of animal behaviour or human behaviour and social organisation from a biological perspective.

expected-experience environment: The neurologists Greenough and Black (1992), talking about early brain development describe one aspect as experience-expectant, that is, development that will not happen unless a particular experience occurs during its critical period.

experience-dependent: The ability of the brain to modify itself and adapt to challenges of the environment is referred to as plasticity. Plasticity can be categorised as experience-expectant or experience-dependent. Experience-expectant plasticity refers to the integration of environmental stimuli into the normal patterns of development.

expressive: Generally means showing feelings or emotions.

expressive movements/pre-reaching movements: Movements that manifest themselves during various (particularly emotional) psychological states and that serve as their external expression. The most important class of expressive movements is represented in mimicry and pantomime. In the broadest sense expressive movements include all shadings of the voice and intonations conveying emotions, as well as the autonomic reactions that accompany these emotions – vascular, respiratory and secretory. In infants such movements can be seen even before the baby is able to reach out.

gestural/gestural hand movements: A movement of the limbs or body made to express or help express thoughts or to emphasise speech. The action of making such a motion or motions.

grammar: The whole system and structure of a language or of languages in general, usually taken as consisting of syntax and morphology (including inflections) and sometimes also phonology and semantics.

gnosis: Means knowledge.

guided participation: A term first used by Barbara Rogoff to refer to how children actively acquire new skills and capacities through their active participation in meaningful activities (like planting, cooking and so on) alongside parents and other more experienced companions.

habitus: First used by Pierre Bourdieu, it refers to a system of embodied dispositions or tendencies that organise the ways in which individuals perceive the social world around them and react to it.

head–eye coordination: Changing the direction of the line of sight is essential for the visual exploration of our environment.

hierarchical: Arranged or ranked in order such as first and last or smallest to biggest.

human sense: A term first development by Margaret Donaldson explaining that young children need to see the purpose of any problem in order to be able to solve it or have any emotional response to it.

imprints: Literally it can mean to impress or stamp (a mark or outline) on a surface, or in zoological terms a young animal will come to recognise another animal, person or thing as a parent or other object of habitual trust.

infant-directed speech: Adults in most parts of the world speak to infants differently from how they speak to others. When talking to babies they use a high-pitched tone and elongated words in an exaggerated manner with much facial expressiveness. This kind of speech is also known as motherese, parentese or baby talk.

innate: Natural or born with.

integrated motor system: Motor control is the process by which humans and animals use their brain/cognition to activate and coordinate the muscles and limbs involved in the performance of a motor skill. Fundamentally, it is the integration of sensory information, both about the world and the current state of the body, to determine the appropriate set of muscle forces and joint activations to generate some desired movement or action. This process requires cooperative interaction between the central nervous system and the musculo-skeletal system, and is thus a problem of information processing, coordination, mechanics, physics and cognition. Successful motor control is crucial to interacting with the world, not only determining action capabilities, but regulating balance and stability as well.

intent participation learning: In intent participation, learners engage collaboratively with others in the social world.

intentional conscious agent: Agency means being in control of one's movements or actions, decisions or choices. Being an intentional conscious agent means being responsible for what you do as a whole.

interactional synchrony: Interactional synchrony refers to how a parent's speech and infant's behaviour become finely synchronised so that they are in direct response to one another. It was defined by Feldman (2007) as a 'temporal coordination of micro-level social behaviour' and as 'symbolic exchanges between parent and child'.

intermental vs intramental: Intramental ability exists within the child while intermental ability occurs in the relationship between people. When a parent gives meaning to the communication of their child when that child is unable to do so for herself the parent is working in the child's zone of proximal development.

internal representation: A mental or cognitive representation, in philosophy of mind, cognitive psychology, neuroscience and cognitive science is a hypothetical internal cognitive symbol that represents external reality.

interpersonal coordination: The tendency for individuals to implicitly synchronise their behavioural and linguistic communication patterns during social interactions.

intersubjectivity: The philosophy dictionary offers this concise definition, which pleases me: existing between conscious minds; shared by more than one conscious mind.

intonation: There are two related meanings: the first refers to speech and means inflection, pitch, tone, timbre, cadence, cadency, lilt, rise and fall, modulation, speech pattern; the second refers to music as in the accuracy of pitch in playing or singing.

kinaesthetic: The sense that detects changes in bodily position or weight, due to movement of the muscles, tendons and joints.

knowing with sight: Means visual gnosis or knowledge.

language acquisition: Children acquire language through a subconscious process during which they are unaware of grammatical rules. They get a feel for what is and what isn't correct. In order to acquire language, the learner needs a source of natural communication.

language development: Language learning, on the other hand, is not communicative. It is the result of direct instruction in the rules of language.

language learning: This term implies that language does not arise through normal communication between people but through the learner being given the rules and the vocabulary.

lexical meaning: The meaning of a word considered in isolation from the sentence containing it and regardless of its grammatical context.

mediation: A key term used by Vygotsky to describe how children learn through interactions with others. In its stricter Vygotskian sense, mediation involves the use of cultural tools, such as books, music, paintings, computers, pens and pencils – utterances in spoken or sign language, in coming to know their cultural worlds.

metaphoric: A figure of speech in which a word or phrase is applied to something to which it is not literally applicable in order to suggest something felt or resembled.

mimesis: This is an important term with a range of meanings, which include imitation, representation, mimicry and more.

mirror neuron system: A group of specialised neurons that 'mirrors' the actions and behaviour of others.

morphological: The size, shape and structure of an organism or one of its parts.

morphogenesis: The biological process that causes an organic life system to develop its shape and function.

motherese: The ways in which mothers or other primary caregivers speak to their babies. See infant-directed speech.

movement neuroscience: In essence this means the links between the brain and movement or the science of neural systems that generate and regulate movements.

mutual entrainment: Difficult to define but sometimes used to mean the manner in which changes in specific components of parenting are sequenced and become reciprocally reinforcing (or mutually entrained) to engender and sustain the cascade of long-term beneficial effects resulting from postnatal depression.

narrative form: Narrative means story, so narrative form would be something with a beginning, a middle and an end.

narrative of motor activity: The observation and recording in story form of the development of movement.

narrative structure: Means the same as narrative form.

neonatologist: Someone who studies the newborn child, the neonate.

neurochemical: It means of or relating to neurochemistry or it can refer to (of a drug or other substance) affecting the nervous system.

neuropsychology: Neuropsychology studies the structure and function of the brain as they relate to specific psychological processes and behaviors. It is an experimental field of psychology that aims to understand how behaviour and cognition are influenced by brain functioning and is concerned with the diagnosis and treatment of behavioural and cognitive effects of neurological disorders. Whereas classical neurology focuses on the physiology of the nervous system and classical psychology is largely divorced from it, neuropsychology seeks to discover how the brain correlates with the mind.

ontogenesis: The biological definition is the development of an individual organism or anatomical or behavioural feature from the earliest stage to maturity.

organogenesis: The biological definition is the production and development of the organs of an animal or plant. Can you see from this definition and the one above that genesis means progression?

ostensive: Ostensive means of, relating to or constituting definition by exemplifying the thing or quality being defined. That is not very helpful so try this one. It is usually accompanied with a gesture pointing out the object serving as an example, and for this reason is also often referred to as 'definition by pointing'. Ostensive definitions rely on an analogical or case-based reasoning by the subject they are intended to educate or inform.

ostensive marking: Difficult to define but would suggest that it is finding ways of making the meaning clear by using gesture, pointing, utterances and other verbal and non-verbal cues.

paralimbic neocortex: The paralimbic cortex is an area of three-layered cortex in the brain.

parieto-temporal: Concerning the parietal and temporal bones or lobes.

performing: An everyday word meaning to act or show others, so involves an audience.

person–person: This is another way of talking of a two way interaction, or a dyadic interaction.

person–person–object: This is a dyadic interaction involving a topic or an object.

perturbation: Means anxiety or mental uneasiness. Tests in infants revealed that they would be distressed when the mother withdrew her attention.

phototherapy: Simply the use of light in the treatment of physical or mental illness.

pitch: As used by Trevarthen, Gratier and Malloch, for example, it refers to the quality of a sound governed by the rate of vibrations producing it; the degree of highness or lowness of a tone.

pitch-plots: A method for showing a graph of the pitch of vocalisations.

polyvagal theory: The polyvagal theory specifies two functionally distinct branches of the vagus, or tenth cranial nerve.

pre-reaching: A movement made by an infant that comes before reaching. The baby will extend her arm and hand towards an object that interests her, but will rarely be able to make hand contact with that object.

precursor: A thing or person that comes before another of the same kind; a forerunner.

primary intersubjectivity: Trevarthen defines this as the capacity for sustained communication demonstrated during early protoconversations.

proto: This is a prefix that means first, earliest, original or primitive.

proto-habitus: Trevarthen says that by three months an intimate attachment with the mother is consolidated by increased playfulness with body movements and sounds, and games with the infant become attractive to the father and other family members as well. The play takes increasingly ritual forms in body games and songs that attract interest and attuned response from the infant. A 'proto-habitus' of performances develops through the first semester, and the infant starts to adapt to the particular cultural forms of body expression and voice, learning to reproduce 'performances' for appreciation. See both proto and habitus.

protoconversations: The very early interactions between infant and caregiver.

protonarratives: Early examples of exchanges between infant and caregiver.

provocations: As used by Trevarthen and others the definition offered here is apt. 'Searching for the mechanism of neonatal imitation resulted in the discovery of neonatal initiative capacity, here called "provocation." Newborns spontaneously produced previously imitated gestures while waiting for the experimenter's response. A psychophysiological analysis revealed that imitation was accompanied by heart rate increase while gesture initiation was accompanied by heart rate deceleration, suggesting different underlying mechanisms. Results imply that infants are not only capable of responding to a model movement by imitating, but that they also have the capacity to provoke an imitative response, thus sustaining an interaction. These findings may constitute a laboratory demonstration of the first dialogue and, according to our hypothetical model, they represent how human imprinting begins' (Nagy & Molnar 2004).

psychobiology: The branch of science that deals with the biological basis of behaviour and mental phenomena.

psychopharmacology: The branch of psychology concerned with the effect of drugs on the mind and behaviour.

psychophysiological: Is the branch of physiology that is concerned with the relationship between mental (psyche) and physical (physiological) processes; it is the scientific study of the interaction between mind and body.

pulse: An everyday word related to the blood in our veins but used by Trevarthen and others to refer to the rhythmic patterns of speech and music.

quality: Another everyday word but used by Trevarthen to show sensitivity for the temporal variation in intensity, pitch and timbre of voices and of instruments that mimic the human voice.

referential gestures: Humans commonly use referential gestures that direct the attention of recipients to particular aspects of the environment. Because the recipient of a referential gesture must infer the signaller's meaning, the use of these gestures has been linked with cognitive capacities such as the ability to recognise another individual's mental state.

reflective thinking: Reflective thinking is a part of the critical thinking process referring specifically to the processes of analysing and making judgements about what has happened.

resolution: This often means the end of something or the answer to a puzzle.

right hemisphere: Each hemisphere of the brain is dominant for particular behaviours. It appears that the right brain is dominant for spatial abilities, face recognition, visual imagery and music. The left brain may be more dominant for calculations, maths and logical abilities.

scaffolding: Scaffolding is an often-used construct to describe the ongoing support provided to a learner by an expert. Thus, when a child (or a novice) learns with an adult or a more capable peer, the learning occurs within the child's zone of proximal development (ZPD).

secondary intersubjectivity: At about nine months there is a change in the infant's motives and interests that starts cooperative practical learning beginning the endless game of sharing cultural meanings, tools and jobs to do (Trevarthen & Hubley 1978). The baby's curiosity about what other people are doing, and the things they use, leads to following directives, trying to make conventional messages and trying to use objects properly – as tools. This is vital preparation for learning language to name meanings.

sharing behaviours: A common sense definition is that two or more people look and listen to one another and cooperate and collaborate on tasks.

social sensitivity: Is the personal ability to perceive, understand and respect the feelings and viewpoints of others, and it is said to be reliably measurable.

socionoesis: The loss of collective story-making.

spectrograph: A spectrograph is an instrument that separates light into a frequency spectrum and records the signal using a camera. There are several kinds of machines referred to as spectrographs, depending on the precise nature of the waves.

spectrographic analysis: This is a process in sensor technology in which chemical elements are determined by measuring the wavelengths or spectral line intensity of a sample of matter.

split brains: Split brain is a lay term to describe the result when the corpus callosum connecting the two hemispheres of the brain is severed to some degree. It is an association of symptoms produced by disruption of or interference with the connection between the hemispheres of the brain.

structure: An everyday word that means how something is put together or made up.

subjectivity: Subjectivity refers to how someone's judgement is shaped by personal opinions and feelings instead of outside influences. Subjectivity is partially responsible for why one person loves an abstract painting while another person hates it.

symbolic: In everyday use it means representing something else.

syntax: The sequence in which words are put together to make a sentence. In English the usual sequence is subject, verb and object.

timbre: Is the perceived sound quality of a musical note, sound or tone that distinguishes different types of sound production.

timing: For Trevarthen, timing, pitch and quality are key.

triadic: Refers to a group of three.

trimester: Three months of gestation.

vagus: Each of the tenth pair of cranial nerves, supplying the heart, lungs, upper digestive tract and other organs of the chest and abdomen.

video motion capture: Capturing images in sequence allowing for detailed analysis.

visual gnosis: The ability to visually recognise various elements and attribute meaning to them (objects, faces, places and colours).

vitality affects: The vitality affects are the affects of attunement, intersubjectivity and social connection: they both express it and are vehicles for their entrainment. As a function of their ephemeral and fluid nature, they are well suited to dyadic coordination and mutual affective sharing.

volume: A measure of the loudness or intensity of a sound.

Note: I apologise if the definitions are sometimes almost as difficult to decode as the words themselves.

Introduction

The life and ideas of Colwyn Trevarthen

I knew very little about Trevarthen's life before I went up to meet him in Edinburgh earlier last year when we spent a fascinating few hours together discussing our shared interests in babies, young children and music; deploring what educators in England were proposing young children must learn; celebrating some of the good practice in terms of early childhood we had both encountered and sharing our responses to the long dark days of winter when both of us had grown up in the southern hemisphere. I came away knowing more about his ideas but very little about his life. He is an intensely private man.

He told me that he was born in Auckland, New Zealand. His father was a patent lawyer who helped inventors and who joined up during the First World War but missed all of the action. He was a creative man – an inventor who made furniture and jewellery. His mother, the oldest of nine children, was a violinist and a liberal intellectual. He has one sister, Jane, now living in California, who pursues an active interest in molecular biology, after working with Linus Pauling at Caltech.

He went to school in New Zealand and completed his first degree in botany and zoology at Auckland University and went on to study the morphological and physiological adaptations of a marine alga called *Hormosira* for his MSc in plant ecology while also studying zoology. From there he moved on to Otago University where he studied animal behaviour or ethology and took courses in physiology and neuroscience at the medical school. Like us all, he was influenced by the gifted teachers he encountered along his very unusual educational pathway. He was and remains curious and eager to be inventive and even today is still asking questions, trying things out, finding solutions with no fear of being thought of as being eccentric. In an interview for the journal *Psychobabble*, he said:

> *Right from my early years in New Zealand I had very good teachers; one got me interested in plant ecology in Auckland, another – my PhD supervisor Roger Sperry in California – got me interested in physiology and the way the brain works.*
>
> (*Psychobabble* 2012: 4)

One person to have had a decisive influence over Trevarthen's career was Archie McIntyre, professor of Physiology at the University of Otago, who suggested that he should apply to do a PhD with Roger Sperry. McIntyre was a physiologist and an ecologist – described by many as a gentle and supportive educator gifted at supporting curiosity about the nature of essential life processes. Already interested in plants and animals, Trevarthen was rapidly becoming interested in both physiology and ecology and the work of Freud on the physiology of emotions. Following McIntyre's advice about new work in psychology and the brain he went on to Caltech (the California Institute of Technology, Pasadena) to work with Roger Sperry and his colleagues. They were working on 'split brains', in which the main direct nerve fibre connections linking the cerebral hemispheres had been surgically cut.

The results of these studies later led to Roger Sperry being awarded the Nobel Prize in Physiology and Medicine in 1981 for his discoveries concerning the functional specialisation of the hemispheres. The initial studies were made with cats and monkeys, which survived the operation with most of their mental functions intact, then the same operation was used to stop the spread of seriously damaging epileptic activity from one cortex to the other of human beings. At that time the only treatment for people suffering from a special kind of epilepsy was to cut off the connection – the corpus callosum – between the two hemispheres. This had allowed Sperry to demonstrate that the left and right hemispheres are specialised so that the left side of the brain normally specialises in the analytical and verbal or rational and the right half in the affective context of space perception and music, for example.

Sperry was cited as the second of the four people who had influenced Trevarthen's early decisions about what academic and intellectual path he wanted to follow. In his work for his PhD with Sperry he developed methods to test eye–hand coordination and visual consciousness and his doctoral thesis was on double visual learning in the two hemispheres of macaque monkeys.

In 1963, at the completion of this work, he received a USPHS (United States Public Health Service) Post-Doctoral Studentship, which allowed him to go to Marseille to the Institut de Neurophysiologie et Psychologie to work with Jacques Paillard, the third great influence on him. Paillard was a specialist in research on how movements are patterned by the nervous system, and he strengthened the role of physiological psychology in the field of movement neuroscience. It was at the University of Marseille that Trevarthen began his professional relationship with Paillard and, aided by him, increased his understanding about how the brain works to invent creative movements of the body. He applied split-brain surgery to study the bimanual (two-handed) motor skills in baboons. These tests showed how the agility of both hands of the monkey could be enhanced by covering one eye so the part of the brain opposite the dominant hand was used, a cross-over that results from the evolution of eyes with lenses that rotate images of the world by 180 degrees.

These studies led to a better appreciation of how delicate use of both hands for clever manipulations could be controlled by sight and touch.

In 1966, on his way to a research fellowship at Harvard, Colwyn travelled to England with a Fellowship in Psychology at Cambridge University, where he worked with Oliver Zangwill, Nicholas Humphrey and Lawrence Weiskrantz on the imagination of visual gnosis or 'knowing' with sight. He eventually found his way to Harvard to work with Jerome Bruner, whom many of you reading this book will have heard of or read about. This came about as a consequence of a visit Professor Jerome Bruner made to Paillard's laboratory to catch up on recent discoveries about how the brain directs body movements with skill. He was interested in the high-speed film studies of hand movements developed by Trevarthen.

Bruner, born blind, died during my writing of this book. He had been influential and much loved, and was interested in connecting psychology with learning and in the creation and use of culture. Trevarthen said:

> *He was one of the founders of the cognitive revolution but he immediately undermined it by setting up an infancy research lab because infants don't really follow the rules. That's pretty 'Bruneresque' behaviour, he's provocative and has always been ahead of the game. He was an incredible teacher and that's where I began the work on infants.*
>
> (*Psychobabble* 2012: 4)

In 1967, with the guidance of Bruner at the Centre for Cognitive Studies and the wonderful facilities for film recordings, the use of spectrographs and other tools for observing and recording the interactions, intentions and decisions of infants, Trevarthen began the journey for which he is best known. He followed the head and eye movements of babies tracking and locating objects and their mastery of hand movements for reaching and grasping. He found common rhythms of coordination.

Trevarthen had journeyed from New Zealand to the United States and then to France, and from looking at ecology and plants and living creatures, to thinking about the role of movement and vision in infancy when he became involved in the world of babies and toddlers. His work with Bruner was important, and, he says

> *it was definitely in a biological – even medical – framework, in the sense of collaborating with paediatrician Berry Brazelton and Martin Richards, an expert on maternal behaviour of hamsters. The three of us set up a recording studio with very good facilities and we made documentary films, which are still being studied. That got me thoroughly involved with the idea of the infant as a being with all sorts of adaptations for human cultural learning, including the ability to transmit ideas via complex body movements which would eventually turn into speech.*
>
> (*Psychobabble* 2012: 4–5)

In that same interview he talked of the interesting and controversial people he met at the Centre for Cognitive Studies in Harvard while he was there. Jean Piaget, for example, came to Cambridge but was dismissive of Bruner and his work. Trevarthen was surprised by Piaget's neglect of the child's motives for communicating feeling and discovery.

By training Trevarthen was a scientist with a knowledge of neurophysiology, particularly of movement and vision. But he also knew about psychology and development, about culture and language. He had learned not only how to make films but also how to analyse them frame by frame to make sense of what was happening. When asked in the interview for the journal *Psychobabble* what had happened next he explained: '*I also noticed that infant movements to objects were different from their movements to people. So we got the idea of the baby as an intentional, conscious agent with the capacity to make well organised movements*' (*Psychobabble* 2012: 5). Many of you will have come across the work of Piaget and will know that such an idea would have been anathema to him. He had described the time after birth as 'the sensorimotor-stage', during which infants are not conscious of objects. It is important to note that Piaget's thinking had been revolutionary in developmental psychology in that he was the first to give babies what Trevarthen calls a concept-making agency. He saw the young child as an active learner or inventor, exploring objects and their properties with 'pleasure in mastery' for themselves.

Trevarthen found young babies to be self-conscious actors or 'show offs', able to imagine performing for other persons, wanting to share life with them without having to know them 'objectively' as objects to be used. This may be quite a difficult concept to take hold of, but keep reading. For Trevarthen, infants have imaginative preparation for how to act in the future with a complex body that shows playful feelings and that is what he calls subjectivity – to be a subject. We will go into this in much more detail later in the book. It was through the examination of film clips of mother and baby interacting that Trevarthen and his colleagues noticed that while very young babies were making lots of expressive movements when interacting with the mother, their movements when looking at an object were less expressive, more focused. This suggested that babies have two kinds of adaptations – one for getting information about objects in the outside world, and possibly trying to get hold of them. Trevarthen called movements like this 'pre-reaching' – that is, an arm and hand movement that has the outline of a coordinated act to pick up an object before the baby can actually reach out far enough to get the object. The other adaptation, aimed at interacting with the mother, was marked by the fact that the baby made many gestural hand movements and used sounds and vocal and facial expressions to engage with and sometimes lead the mother into dialogue. He noted from his analysis of film that in this intersubjectivity – the subjectivity shared between mother and infant – the mothers were often imitating the babies and not the other way around. Intersubjectivity is one of the key concepts he developed and there is more about it later in this book.

Primary intersubjectivity – where the baby is capable of regulating a dialogue so that she becomes the leader or story-teller became the subject of a paper he wrote in 1979.

You may remember the interest Trevarthen had developed in movement from his earlier work with Paillard, who had observed and was impressed by the ways in which animals calibrate their movements by anticipating how they will feel. For generations it had been thought that the movements of babies are 'random' or reflex responses without conscious control. He queried this and found some classical neonatologists like Gordon Avery who agreed that the movements of newborn animals are not random and neither are the movements of humans. In fact, movements of newborn infants may be very adaptive for sharing consciousness. We are, as a species, born more immature than other animals, but are not born as helpless blobs. The human infant is more dependent on the support of the mother or other primary caregiver, but is also capable of showing her own initiative. This idea – that of the human infant being a purposeful and conscious agent – was very new in developmental psychology of the 1960s, and sometimes still strikes people who are educated to be very rational as being questionable.

Trevarthen studied head–eye coordination using the new equipment that allowed for very accurate recordings of the head and eye rotations of babies. Using these he was able to show that very young babies are well coordinated in the way in which they move their eyes and their head. He also saw that the arm and hand movements of babies were very regular and connected to the head–eye movements. It was clear that the babies had an integrated motor system, which is capable of whole body activity. Infants see things in the outside world and make their body act in orientation to them.

Another of Trevarthen's interests, developed from the study of infants with the help of expert musician Stephen Malloch, is in the innate musicality of our sharing of experience, and this has attracted interest, approval and some criticism. Communicative musicality is a way of communication, of the expression of feelings and of dealing with issues and questions of intimate personal relationships. Trevarthen sees musicality as being innate and possessing both aesthetic and moral quality. He says:

> Now we're interested in the fact that babies are extremely sensitive to the subtle balance between aggressive teasing and joyful and friendly sharing of pleasure. It's also, by the way, very important to see the difference in musicality between a mother who is psychotic and a mother who is happy and well. A mother with postnatal depression or psychosis lacks musicality, and she doesn't have a musical communication with her baby. This doesn't make sense to people who don't know what you mean by musicality, so we have been very careful to define the parameters, deriving them from what we see in mother-infant communication and people have found them useful. They find that they can use the parameters we've discovered to give a clearer picture of what's going on when communication is very good or when

it's failing. I suppose there is a core (I don't know what to call them – it could be 'core' or 'corps') of people who don't like anything which is in the slightest bit imaginative. I'm attracted to risky intuitions because I think we've got to try and get some grasp on the intrinsic vitality in organisms – particularly in human experience – and not all the time be trying to measure its practicality.

(*Psychobabble* 2012: 6)

Trevarthen's has been a long and productive life and what sets him apart from many others is the rigorous training in subjects so seemingly remote from the more traditional career and academic routes followed by those interested in and working with young children – such as psychology, child development and education. By the time he arrived at babies he already knew a huge amount about plants and animals, movement and the brain and the importance of being able to document and analyse what he saw and heard.

Summary

This introduction to his life and work and those who influenced him offers you an overview of how Colwyn Trevarthen developed his interests from physiology to neurophysiology, from plants and animals to human infants and, on this journey, developed powerful arguments for just how brilliant babies are. As you will see, some of this information was gleaned from an interview with him by journalists producing *Psychobabble*, Issue 4. If you are interested in reading the whole interview you can find it online (www.think.psy.ed.ac.uk/wp-content/uploads/2015/11/Psychobabble_issue4.pdf).

Section I

From foetus to neonate

When I started writing this book I could not decide exactly where to begin. Trevarthen is very easy to understand face to face and in the presentations he makes to conferences. But since he writes primarily for an academic audience his writing is sometimes difficult to decode. He often writes in collaboration with colleagues and sometimes this adds to the complexity of the language. And because of the breadth of his experience and interests he sometimes uses a very specialist vocabulary.

After grappling with a range of choices I chose to structure the book so that we are looking at Trevarthen's key ideas about development from gestation through to the age of three. So my focus in this first section will be initially on the foetus but then on the infant in the first weeks after birth. As you will see when you read the first small chapter in this section, Trevarthen is not mentioned. He, like the foetus, must wait.

From conception to birth

In this first chapter of the section on foetus and neonate we look at what is known about the development in utero in the first, second and third trimesters. This chapter offers a very simplified version of what happens between conception and birth.

The first trimester

You will know that it takes nine months for a baby to develop inside the mother's womb. We all start out as a microscopic ball of cells that keep on dividing and dividing until the ball of cells has organised itself into three layers known as germ layers. There is an inner layer called the endoderm; a middle layer called the mesoderm; and an outer layer called the ectoderm. It is from these three germ layers that all the organs and tissues of the body will come. The ectoderm will form the outer components of the body, such as skin, hair, and mammary glands, as well as part of the nervous system. Following gastrulation, a section of the ectoderm folds inward, creating a groove that closes and forms an isolated tube down the dorsal midsection of the embryo. This process of neurulation forms the neural tube, which gives rise to the central nervous system. During neurulation, ectoderm also forms a type of tissue called the neural crest, which helps to form structures of the face and brain. The endoderm produced during gastrulation will form the lining of the digestive tract, as well as that of the lungs and thyroid. For animals with three germ layers, after the endoderm and ectoderm have formed, interactions between the two germ layers induce the development of mesoderm. The mesoderm forms skeletal muscle, bone, connective tissue, the heart, and the urogenital system. Drawn from the work of Kate MacCord (2013).

This all happens through cell differentiation. The cells receive signals from your genes in your DNA inside each cell. These genes operate something like an instruction manual: they tell the cell where to go and what to do. Some will become heart cells, others brain cells and yet others nerve cells. Once a cell has been differentiated it cannot change into a different kind of cell. What happens next is called organogenesis and this is where the differentiated cells organise themselves into tissues and organs. In 1972 Maturana coined the term 'auto-poesis' made up of the words 'auto' meaning self and 'poeisis' meaning creation or productivity to define living systems as self-creating (Maturana & Verala 1972/1980). By being self-creating, or autopoeitic, each living system can be said to have and be a way of 'knowing'. Cognition, in the broadest sense of the word, is synonymous with living.

It is in the second month or weeks five to eight that changes become apparent. By week five the embryo changes shape and size. A tiny bump that will become the head appears, together with limb buds that will become arms and legs. The sense organs like the eyes and ears begin to develop. The beginnings of the circulation, nervous, digestive and respiratory systems appear and, at around six weeks, the heart starts pumping blood around the body. In week eight sexual differentiation begins with gonads developing into testes or ovaries. How big do you think the embryo is by the end of this trimester? My sources say about the size of a raspberry.

The second trimester

The second trimester covers months four, five and six (or weeks 13–26). At the beginning of this trimester the tiny foetus has her own fingerprints and her teeth are beginning to develop. There is evidence that she is already moving the muscles in her face to show facial expressions. Her brain has four cerebral lobes and by the end of the fourth month her endocrine system has starting producing most of the hormones we produce as adults. The foetus is becoming more and more active, moving her limbs and head and the mother can feel all of this. By the beginning of the fifth month (weeks 18–22) most of the basic development has taken place. What is needed is refinement. Much of this relates to that most amazing of organs – the eye. During this month the retina develops the distinct layers needed for seeing. And there are refinements in the brain as well as it grows in complexity. Neurons carry on differentiating to take on different jobs within the brain. Whilst this is taking place the body of the foetus is adapting to the mother's daily cycles and this means that its body movements, heart rate and breathing patterns follow daily circadian rhythms. Hair begins to grow on the scalp of the foetus. This trimester is a period of rapid growth and the foetus will be about the size of a peach halfway through it.

The third trimester

Much of the development has been completed but certain refinements are still needed to prepare the foetus for leaving the womb. During the seventh month the wrinkly foetus begins to add layers of fat, and the eyes, which now have eyelashes, begin to open. As the next month starts the photoreceptors in the eyes begin to be able to distinguish light from dark. Only after birth will vision improve so that the infant can see colours and learn to focus. Developments are taking place in the ears too so that the foetus can differentiate high from low sounds. Also during this month the brain and nervous system protect themselves by forming layers of an insulation-type of material called myelin. This is laid down around the axons of the neurons and its function is to increase the speed with which neurons can communicate with one another. The lungs begin to develop air pockets called alveoli. It is these that will help the baby breathe after birth. Inside the womb the baby is moving – touching the wall of the uterus, kicking, bending and stretching her legs, sometimes turning somersaults. She is almost ready to be born and it has been suggested that she has become the size of a decent pineapple.

Summing up

You will appreciate that this is a very simplified guide to the development of the foetus. It is an overture to the rest of the book. If you are very fortunate you might find a copy of the book *The Facts of Life: A Three-Dimensional Study* by Jonathan Miller and David Pelham published in 1984 by Jonathan Cape Limited.

From moving to meaning

Wordless narratives

In this chapter we look at how the newborn baby sets out to engage with others in her world – usually the mother – using all the things she has been practising in utero: looking, listening, touching and moving.

Thinking about movement

Trevarthen and Delafield-Butt adopt a stance that is very different from that of most traditional educationalists (Delafield-Butt & Trevarthen 2013; Trevarthen & Delafield-Butt 2015). But then they are both primarily scientists rather than educationalists. They insist that we are more like animals than has been recognised and that to understand how we have developed as a species requires us to acknowledge this. If we accept that we are animals, it is clear that we are the most mobile, imaginative and cooperative; the most talkative and emotionally expressive. The importance of this for us is that we can learn about ourselves by knowing more about animals. This is an understanding rooted in biology and physiology. If you are particularly interested in this do read the fascinating article written by Trevarthen and Delafield-Butt entitled *Biology of Shared Experience and Language Development* (2013).

We know that both animals and humans move for a purpose. They need or desire or fear something and are able to coordinate their muscle actions to achieve their goals and to protect themselves from harm. When you think about it even the simplest act – perhaps to reach out and touch something – must be governed by thinking ahead and then carrying out a sequence of actions to achieve something or avoid trouble. So movement is both *intentional* and *goal-directed*. Some actions are automatic responses, for example to pull back from pain. Even whilst still in the womb, the foetus moves from general movements to more focused ones.

 Think about this

By ten weeks' gestational age the foetus is able to move her limbs separately from her torso and her hand movements may become directed at parts of her own body. In the second trimester we noted that the foetus could make purposeful movements. The use of four-dimensional ultrasound reveals that in the third trimester the *foetus makes facial expressions showing evidence of feelings* and *forms positions of the mouth as if in preparation for speech sounds.* So there is evidence that whilst the human infant is still in the womb she makes expressive movements and gestures suggesting both self-awareness and intelligent planning.

Is there anything about this finding that surprises you? What surprised me was that expressive movements and gestures occur so early in development.

In more recent work, Delafield-Butt and Trevarthen (2015) say that the movements of animals and humans are organised into graceful, discreet and rhythmic sequences, each with its own purpose or goal. If you have ever had the joy of seeing animals in the wild you will understand what they mean by this. I was lucky enough to have been born in South Africa where trips to see game were regular and wonderful annual events and I can remember crying at the beautiful sight of an owl swooping out of a night sky. The significance of all this for us is that movement is *goal-directed, purposeful, expressive and built up of a sequence of carefully coordinated actions.* Why this matters to us is that this is the foundation for what Trevarthen goes on to tell us about the relationship of movement to narrative. Our gestures enable us, from very early in life, to create a cultural world, unique to human beings where motives are shared in narrations of movement expressing our thoughts and feelings. Trevarthen is quoted as saying that '*gestural expressions, with their innate timing and combination in narrations, are the foundation for learning all the forms and values of the elaborate cultural rituals and the conventions of art and language*' (Gentilucci & Corballis 2006: 949–960).

Tiny narratives and cultural tools

The human infant recognises her mother as someone essential to her life before birth. She has, after all, heard this voice over the nine months growing inside the womb. The powerful evidence that has been gathered through the analysis of newborn babies communicating with the mother or other caregiver tells us that the baby is born with the *expectancy of human company.*

Trevarthen and others have gathered wonderful examples, illustrating this expectancy of human company.

For example, in 1986, Gunilla Preisler filmed five-month old Maria, born blind, conducting her mother singing. The films of Maria show her lying on her back whilst her mother is bottle feeding her and singing her two Swedish songs which the baby has come to know well. From time to time the baby joins in by waving her left hand in graceful waves. Using sophisticated recording and measuring devices it was seen that the baby's 'conducting' preceded a change in the emotional quality of the mother's singing by 300 milliseconds. It was as though the baby was actually conducting the mother in her song.

This is the first example in this book of a film clip analysed by Trevarthen and you will encounter other examples throughout the book and may well encounter this one again because the analyses are so complex and varied they are cited again and again.

Trevarthen uses the word narrative for the mini-dialogues that the newborn infant engages in with her mother or other caregiver. The word is used with a particular meaning to illustrate that the baby is using all the means she has in order to join with her mother through an act of communication. The act itself may take only seconds but it is the start of the baby becoming a member of her own community and culture. We find in Trevarthen's work the influence of Bruner, who wrote in depth about the role of narrative in our lives and insisted that narrative is the way in which we organise our experiences and our memories, account for our reasons for doing things or not doing them, make our excuses or explanations and hold our beliefs and values. He said that narrative or 'story-telling' is one of the most powerful forms of human communication and added that narrative structure is built into social interactions even before the development of spoken language. In analysing the seemingly simple protoconversations newborn babies have with their mothers, Trevarthen notes that the mother vocalises and the baby responds, but the baby clearly does not yet have any spoken language. So we have compositions of wordless communication, which Trevarthen calls narratives. Bruner called a protoconversation (analysed and named by Mary Catherine Bateson) a little narrative.

In our narratives we both develop and use what Vygotsky called cultural tools, which may be real tools but also the things made from and with these tools. So cultural tools can be things like pens and pencils, books and computers, violins and paintbrushes. The cultural tools may be universal but more commonly are particular to the culture in which they are developed. The narratives we make are made within our cultures and transmitted culturally through the use of cultural tools and the people we encounter. Narratives can be seen as versions of a reality that we make up.

 Think about this

Gratier and Trevarthen (2008) tell us that:

> *Narrative is most often considered a language-based way of telling a story, and studies of verbal narrative, including both written and oral forms of "telling", are typically concerned with elements of structure, coherence-producing linguistic devices and individual modes of production.*

(123–124)

To enable you to really think about this you may need help in decoding some of the specialist words in this statement.

Structure, you will know, is how the story goes and in its simplest form it has a beginning, a middle and an end. A coherence-producing linguistic device is a very complicated way of saying that the language is used in a way to allow the listener or reader to understand. Individual modes of production mean that everyone will tell a story differently. The authors are talking here primarily of verbal narratives. But narratives do not have to be verbal. Think about dance, mime, painting, music, for example, all of which communicate ideas and feelings without using words, spoken or written.

We are accustomed to thinking of narratives/stories being either written or oral, but rarely of being only physically presented (as through dance and mime, in music and paintings). To understand Trevarthen's findings we need to consider what is meant by a narrative without words. It is tempting to think of narrative or story as something entertaining, rather than seeing it, as Bruner did, as the fundamental way by which we remember and reflect on our experiences and then share these with others. In this sharing we may engage in elaboration, alteration, invention, comparison, personalising and more. When we tell our stories to others we are sharing not only what we have done or said or made but also what we have imagined or invented for our pleasure. In narratives there may be considerations of what has already happened and what might happen in the future; the story might relate to real or imagined events or people. It is a cognitive and a social and creative act and it is fascinating to consider that it is what the human infant does from the moment of birth. So essentially *narrative means making and sharing meaning*. Through their earliest interactions infants start to make stories using what they can do – move, watch, listen, copy, initiate, feel and express, invent and elaborate. So when we think about narratives in this context we are thinking about non-verbal interactive narrative.

Examples can be found on YouTube, where you can see film clips of infants 'performing' just such stories. Trevarthen has a wonderful film clip of a baby, less than an hour after birth, watching and imitating hand movements, and another of six-month-old Emma sitting on her father's knee and, when her mother says 'Clap handies', she performs the clapping movements to the camera with a huge smile on her proud face.

Here is a photograph of my first granddaughter Hannah performing a trick she had just mastered – wrinkling her nose – to the huge appreciation of her mother.

Towards protoconversations

After birth the baby begins to engage in interactions with the primary caregiver – usually the mother – and at about two months she is taking turns in vocalisations and gestures. By three to four months the baby has become more playful and cheeky and the mother has to try harder to engage her interest. Through the familiar shared action games and rituals, jokes and songs and rhymes in which the baby participates the foundations for speech are being laid. Single intentions become organised to achieve more complex goals. The baby copies the actions of others, is inducted into the cultural practices of her community and through early protoconversations and collaborative play and hearing the talk of others around her the baby encounters and then uses the narrative form of introduction, development, climax and resolution.

 Think about this

To illustrate what is known as the narrative form, here is a spoken story told by four-year-old Octavia:

> *Once upon a time when I was little in my garden there were a earthworm coming out of my plant.*

The introduction is *Once upon a time*; the development *when I was little*; the climax *there were a earthworm* and the resolution *coming out of my plant.* Octavia is no longer a baby and she is verbally telling the story. Trevarthen's findings show us that the interactions between baby and primary caregiver are tiny narratives told through sound, movement, gesture and expression. The making and telling of stories is how we come to know about our world and about the people and events and objects that shape our shared lives.

Trevarthen is clearly not suggesting that infants can tell stories like this with such precise naming of meanings, but their utterances and expressions in their early interactions follow this narrative structure.

What, if anything, surprises you about this?

Attunement

Delafield-Butt recorded the performance of what he called the *narrative of motor activity* in a newborn baby B – one of a pair of twins born prematurely. The babies were in intensive care in the hospital with their mother visiting them every day for a session where she could hold the babies body to body or kangarooing, as it is called. When they were almost able to leave hospital a recording was made. At the time baby B was being oxygenated by a nasal cannula, having had much needed assistance with his breathing from birth. This, understandably, made vocalising more difficult for him. To start with he was still asleep and his mother was asked to wake him up gently. The tiny sample of their dialogue, which is described here, lasted for only roughly 30 seconds. Using motherese the mother began to talk to her tiny baby who responded by showing interest in what she was doing. In turn she followed his responses with responses of her own. The researchers stated that B had been the author of his own story with the mother following his lead.

> *The mother invited him then followed his animation and willingness (to) 'play the game' with her. Their mutual interest in the 'dialog' was sustained by the 'attunement' of the rhythmic vocal invitations of the mother (Stern, 2000), with occasional touches by her gesturing right hand, and by the eagerness of the infant to respond with expressive body movements, hand gestures, attentive looking, smiles, and vocalizations.*
>
> (Delafield-Butt & Trevarthen 2015: 9)

Here is an abbreviated version of the analysis of this tiny incident, following the narrative structure of introduction, development, climax and resolution. What you have just read sets the scene. This is how the researchers recorded and analysed what took place.

Introduction: the first nine seconds (0–9s)
In the first 3 seconds the baby, who had been asleep, began to stir as his mother said, softly 'Are you woken up Mister?' He turned to her with his eyes still closed. His left hand was held shut by his head and his right hand was lying open on the bed. He made a small sound just before his mother said 'Good afternoon!' She then touched his side with her right index finger, then pointed to her mouth in rhythmic synchrony with speech before laying her hand gently on the bed beside him. The baby closed his mouth with his tongue between his lips, then turned away as though to go back to sleep, making a sleepy jerk to face his right hand. His left hand made a fast movement up and to the right to follow the head, and his right hand moved up a little with the fingers opening as his mother started to say, 'Good afternoon, wee B' . Then she turned to face him, placing her right index finger next to him. His right hand opened and shut synchronously with the word 'B' – he was listening. At 7 seconds, as his mother said 'How are you doin?' his right hand moved slightly forward, moved a finger gently, again in synchrony with her speech. She withdrew her finger as she said 'Eh?' and as her voice rose, B smiled and shut his right hand. He was clearly listening and shadowing his mother's speaking with the movements of his right hand.

Development: 10–17 seconds
The introduction ended with the baby smiling and then making a vocalisation. His mouth opened and shut quickly as his mother said: 'Oooh, look at that big smile' and then touched the bed with her finger. B appeared to be swallowing after an attempt to vocalise. His mother was checking on the monitor that he was all right and said, in a different style and tone of voice, 'Oh, that's all great!' B reached up with his right hand and opened his eyes in synchrony with the phrase just uttered and as she said the word 'great' he made a chewing movement and looked at his hand. At 15 seconds his right hand opened and closed and his wrist turned away from his face. His mother tickled him gently and said to him with a lift of intonation 'Look at that big smile!' as she touched the blanket with her finger. B's right hand moved down to touch the blanket.

Climax: 18–22 seconds
As B's mother says 'Hi-ya', he stretches his head up to look forward turning his right hand back at the wrist in a waving gesture, opens his mouth wide and smiles. Then he turns quickly to face his mother, vocalises with a rough sound and gestures smiling and grimacing with the effort. At 19–20s when his mother says 'Hello there!', both his hands are pulled up back and out in a big rowing gesture (J K). As mother's voice glides dramatically down through an octave from C5 to C4 between 20 and 21s B opens his mouth very wide and closes it with a smile in synchrony with fast forward and back down and pulled back rowing movements of his two hands. His eyes open and he coughs at 20s (L). At 22s B makes a second rowing cycle and his mouth shuts. As his mother finishes the vocal glide and turns to her right his hands are at his shoulders and his tongue is visible in an open mouth.

Climax or coda: 23–30 seconds
In this, the denouement of the narrative, B pushed his foot against the mother who said 'Oh, you're kicking your Mum!' He turned his head up at the sound of the word Mum, closed his eyes and and when she more or less repeated what had just happened he seemed to lose interest.

(9–12)

Remember that this is an abbreviated account.

Delafield-Butt was able to record and then analyse through the use of video motion capture. If this interests you put https://www.youtube.com/watch into your search engine, go to YouTube and look for Delafield-Butt talking about infant narrative if it is still online. In his talk he says that it was his basic training in brain development and in how individual cells grow and combine to enable and control how behaviour is patterned that started him on this path.

One of the people who had an influence on Trevarthen was Daniel Stern. Born in Manhattan, Stern completed a first degree in medicine, then carried out psychopharmacology research and later trained as a psychoanalyst. He first came across the work of J. S. Rosenblatt, a doctor who established a reputation for his seminal work on neonates and maternal behaviour. It was for his work on kittens and cats that he earned the title of 'father of mothering' or 'father of maternal behaviour' in the field of psychobiology. In the 1970s Stern began his work of carrying out a microanalysis of mother–infant vocal and gestural communication and showed how this worked reciprocally in the sense that it mattered to both mother and baby who approached their vocal duets with intense engagement. To do this he videotaped babies and studied the tapes second by second. His book *The Interpersonal World of the Infant* (1985) has had a lasting influence in the field of psychotherapy and *Forms of Vitality: Exploring Dynamic Experience in Psychology, the Arts, Psychotherapy and Development* (2010) was of particular interest to Trevarthen. In this book Stern used neuroscience to explain human 'empathy' or feelings for others. You can see from this where their interests coincided. They shared an interest in infant–mother relationships and Stern was particularly interested in what he called vitality affects. Affects, as you may well know, are feelings. Stern observed that the human infant shows evidence of feelings such as intense joy and disgust and, significantly, these are connected with the vital processes of the body – breathing, sleeping and waking, for example. So there is a clear link between emotions and physical state. In effect, what he is saying is that the human infant experiences intense emotions and feelings and that these can arise from and develop in their relationships with others. He talked of the mother–baby relationship as being a biobehavioural system, regulated at brain level through the neurochemical systems and circuits in their human bodies. When the needs of the baby have been satisfied, the baby experiences what Stern calls feelings of vitality. Something triggers the look of joy on the baby's face and whoever else is involved in the interaction is surely smiling too. Thus a system of an expected-experience environment has been created – when the baby has eaten she feels full and expects to feel the same after her next meal. What is becoming evident are the ways in which infants can capture the feelings and intentions of others. And all of this before the development of words and language.

The beginnings of imitation

One of the most astonishing capacities of the newborn baby is that of being able to imitate both the expressions and movements of the human face. The newborn has clearly never seen her own face and so the ability to mimic what is seen on the face of another person involves the baby being able to match what she sees with what she feels with her own facial movements. In addition the baby has to recognise that the person she is looking at and copying is like her in some ways. You will almost certainly have seen examples of the newborn infant mimicking someone who sticks out her tongue. Rhesus monkeys are also capable of doing this. It appears that this imitative facility rests in a special mirror neuron system in the brain and this is what triggers the copying of what is seen.

The debate about neonatal imitation has been going on for years and recordings made in many countries, including those from urban and rural, first- and third-world settings, have given us enough material to be able to state securely that newborn infants do imitate others, everywhere. The evidence also suggests that *imitation requires the infant to engage in self-motivated and intentional behaviour.* In other words the baby does not copy by chance but imitates in a search for establishing contact with others and identifying those they copy as familiar companions. A young doctor, Emese Nagy, who was also qualified as a psychologist and Peter Molnar examined the purposefulness and expectation of imitation in babies of less than two days old (Nagy & Molnar 2004). Nagy started by putting out her tongue, then paused and watched the baby. After sometimes a pause as long as two minutes the infant copied putting out her tongue as a 'provocation'.

 Think about this

In the conclusions to the paper Nagy and Molnar said:

> If the purpose of neonatal initiation is to initiate interaction accompanied by social expectations, then both imitation of a gesture and initiation of a previously imitated gesture are motivated behaviours, and they model the first preverbal human communication in a laboratory setting.
>
> (Nagy & Molnar 2004: 61)

Lynne Murray (once a student of Trevarthen) said:

newborn babies have a fundamental predisposition to respond to social signals and they rapidly develop a specific attraction to their carers. This is matched by similar impulses on the part of the parents, who want to engage with babies generally and their own babies in particular. Specific brain systems are active from birth, helping babies to relate to others and share their experiences. Together these processes ensure that babies and their parents can quickly establish a close connection, and over the first month the foundations are laid for them to begin to communicate socially with each other.

(2014: 10–11)

So here we are at the very heart of the matter. The newborn infant wants to connect with the parents and the parents want to connect with the child. Murray talks of the early fleeting contacts between mother and newborn child and gives as an example Stanley, aged only two weeks old, whose initial contacts with the mother are through touch and eye contact. Yet this tiny baby widens his eyes whilst feeding when his mother starts to stroke his head.

This is how it ought to be and very often is, but we all know of the tragic cases when this is not the reality.

Tracking purposeful behaviour

There is evidence that the human foetus begins to show signs of purposeful movement at about ten weeks in the womb. At this point the movement of arms become distinct from general movements and the foetus is observed to move the hands in order to reach out to parts of the body, especially to the head and face. Alessandra Piontelli (2010) traces how this is followed by purposeful actions of the whole body or by the separate parts. Movies made of the foetus inside the mother's body by four-dimensional ultrasound show it moves in response to cues such as the sound of the mother's voice, and Piontelli observes that a foetus is using reaching and touch movements to discover such things as the presence of a twin, the surface of the wall of the uterus and so on. In the last trimester ultrasound studies by Najda Reissland (e.g. Reissland 2012; Reissland and Kisilevsky 2016) reveal that the facial expressions of the foetus express emotions ranging from pleasure to displeasure and the movements of the lips and mouth suggest adaptations towards being able to make speech sounds.

After birth, through interactions with others, the infant becomes aware not only of self but of others and this is the start of a lifetime of meaning-making and meaning-sharing. This is what Trevarthen calls narrative.

Musical narratives

Communicative musicality

In this chapter we look at how the baby and mother form a strong and binding bond where sounds, movement, rhythm, pitch and tone are used to start and continue a dialogue.

If you think about it in terms of what you have seen or heard or experienced about the interactions between caregivers and infants and toddlers, you may well have noticed that music plays a vital role. Malloch (1999: 29) puts it like this:

> *A mother and her young baby are playfully interacting. We hear the mother speak in short bursts, talking in an inviting sing-song manner, and the baby occasionally 'answers back.' It appears that communication is taking place but based in what? The baby cannot understand the meaning of the words the mother is using, and the baby often answers in 'gliding-type' sounds. The communication must be 'held' by means other than <u>lexical meaning</u>, <u>grammar</u> and <u>syntax</u>.*

How it all began

In 1979 Trevarthen, whilst doing a micro-analysis of video recordings of six-week-old Laura and her mother in his laboratory at Edinburgh University, noticed that the mother joined in with and copied the baby's sounds, modulating these to invite the baby to carry on the dialogue, the narrative or the song. Seventeen years later Stephen Malloch, who was completing a postdoctoral fellowship in psychology with Trevarthen at the University of Edinburgh, heard these duets/conversations and said:

> *As I listened, intrigued by the fluid give and take of the communication, and the lilting speech of the mother as she chatted with her baby, I began to tap my foot. I am, by training, a musician, so I was very used to automatically feeling the beat as I listened to musical sounds ... I replayed the tape, and again I could sense a distinct rhythmicity and melodious give and take to the gentle prompting of Laura's mother and the pitched vocal replies from Laura. ... A few weeks later, as I walked down*

*the stairs to Colwyn's main lab, the words 'communicative musicality' came into
my mind as a way of describing what I had heard.*

(Malloch & Trevarthen 2009: 3–4)

It was the beginning of a long and fruitful collaboration.

 Think about this

Introduction to communicative musicality

In a joint paper published in 2002, Trevarthen and Malloch made some
interesting assertions, which you are invited to consider.

- From the time of birth, infants are able to engage musically with
  parents and caregivers.
- Music is used differently in the stages of an infant's development: first
  to calm and arouse, then to provide an opportunity for performance
  and sharing.
- An infant may learn language patterns by first recognising musical
  patterns in a parent's or caregiver's speech.
- 'Communicative musicality' is a term used to explain using music to
  converse emotionally with others.

(Trevarthen & Malloch 2002: 11)

There is a wealth of scientific information now about mothers singing to their
babies to lull them to sleep or to calm them down, and of mothers who, having
heard the songs themselves from their own mothers, remember them and sing
them to their babies. So, yes, we can be sure that babies are able to engage
musically with their caregiver. And we can accept that music is used for different
purposes. But what allows us to accept that babies learn language patterns by
first recognising musical patterns in a parent's or caregiver's speech? To
understand more about this we need to examine more closely just what it is
that the mother does to draw the baby into the musicality of spoken language.

We have established that from birth the human infant shows eagerness to be in
the company of others. She looks into faces, listens to voices, copies movements
and displays pleasure and pain. Mothers (and fathers or other primary caregivers)
interacting with their babies do not speak to their babies in the ways in which
they talk to one another. They adopt a different, more graceful style of speech
without anyone telling them to do this. They change the <u>pitch</u> and <u>intonation</u>
and <u>cadence</u> of their speech so that it becomes more sing–song and has shorter
utterances, lots of repetition, longer pauses and clearer pronunciation.

Mothers and fathers throughout the world do this in all the languages of the
world. This speech is called 'motherese' or 'parentese' or <u>'infant-directed
speech'</u> (IDS). For some years it was called 'baby talk' and looked down on as

being patronising to the baby. You may remember that Trevarthen, having had music in his life from birth, was a careful and attentive listener and he noticed the particular lilting quality of the vocalisations made by mothers in particular in the earliest days of the life of a baby. He began to use comparison to music or dance to describe the nature or poetry of the language used by the mother and – consequently – by the infant.

Motherese is organised into repeated phrases and Daniel Stern drew attention to the '*dynamic narrative envelopes*' of a mother's utterances with what he called their fluctuating urgency and intensity. I listened to a mother with her newborn baby saying over and over '*big boy, big boy*' to the tiny baby in her arms. It is remarkable to see how newborn babies actively manage to coordinate their gestures and expressions to the mother's sensitive message and they mimic one another's vocalisations in pitch and timbre.

Mary Bateson was a linguist and an anthropologist when she perceived, from work she did with Margaret Bullowa at the Massachusetts Institute of Technology (MIT) in Boston, that protoconversations induct the infant into language and the rhythms and melodies of the popular, religious or traditional practices of the child's culture (Bateson 1979). There is abundant evidence that babies pay more attention to someone using motherese than to someone speaking normally. For Trevarthen and Malloch, music itself can be regarded as narrative without words in the sense that it is sequential – it has a beginning, a development and an ending in its simplest forms and it contains modulations of tension and energy just as a narrative does. It tells a story about itself.

Trevarthen, in his work on the earliest body movements including interactions between the infant and mother or father, noticed how infants make their movements rhythmically from birth. He also noticed that there had been very little study of the timing and shapes of such movements of response in dialogues. He was convinced that music underpins the rhythmic and fluid conversations that newborns have with their mothers. Go to YouTube and look for 'an intimate conversation between a mother and daughter' posted by cmmoyer in August 2008. This offers a truly wonderful example of such a rhythmic and dancing conversation.

There have been numerous experimental studies since the 1970s into just what it is that allows human infants to both perceive and respond to the communicative signals they get from mothers. The evidence shows that infants can discriminate things like the patterns of timing, the pitch of the voice, the volume of the utterance and the timbre of the voice. Remember too that infants pay attention to facial expressions and hand movements in the early months after birth and make their own facial expressions and hand movements to accompany their protoconversations.

We might ask what it is that mothers do to engage their babies so early into dialogues – what are they feeling and what are they displaying? Mother and baby are coming to know one another by building a very emotionally sustaining bond between them, and in this spoken language appears to be superfluous. By

talking of mother and baby coming to deeply know one another we are talking of an understanding that does not rely on words. This early interpersonal bond is very important to the development of the baby. When the mother and baby communicate effectively they are well attuned to the sounds and the physical gestures of one another and this attunement is critical for the well-being of both mother and child.

 Think about this

Some of the experiments into communicative musicality are disturbing. In one such example the mother was asked to keep her face still and expressionless and to remain silent for one minute. What do you think happened?

Tronick *et al.* (1980) tell us that the baby in that situation of getting no verbal or gestural/emotional response from the mother became very distressed. In another example cited by Murray and Trevarthen (1985) a mother and her baby of two months old were able to interact with one another using a video-sound link in which each was photographed by a hidden camera that was set up to allow them to see one another in real time. First a video of the mother reacting as she would normally and positively was shown to the baby. The baby happily responded until there was no replying response from the mother. At that point the baby protested and began to withdraw. The message is clear. Malloch (1999) expresses it like this:

> *This experiment demonstrates how vital it is that an infant receive vocal and gestural responses that fit with its innate predispositions to interact with one another. An infant seeks not just encouraging forms of signal from its mother – the signals must be appropriately timed and inflected.*
>
> (1999: 31)

There are two key words in the statement above and I wonder if you have noticed them and queried their significance. The key words are *innate predispositions*. Innate you will almost certainly know means to be born with and predispositions are the feelings and expectations, the habits of mind that already exist, with a sense of time to share with a companion.

Malloch defined three coordinated dimensions of early musicality, which he called pulse, quality and narrative. These are everyday words but are used in a particular sense with regard to musicality.

- *Pulse* refers to timing and pace of repeating movements. In terms of a piece of music it marks, in steps or stages, the journey from the past to the present to the future, or beginning, middle and end. It is made up of a series of expressive events through time. An event in this context might be a particular sound in a vocal expression perhaps at the beginning or end of a sound, a louder moment or a change in the pitch of the mother's voice.

- *Quality* refers to gestures and sounds that are related to the feelings that are being expressed. So one might call one piece of music peaceful, one furious, one gracious and one jazzy, for example.
- *Narrative* refers to how the gestures and sounds are combined to reflect changing emotions. They allow two people to share a sense of passing time and create what Stern (1993, 1995) called an '*emotional envelope*' throughout this shared time. They express the inner motives for sharing emotion and experience as they create meaning in a joint activity.

The best way to measure pulse is through looking closely at an image revealed in a recording of the event using a spectrograph. When Murray and Trevarthen (1985) analysed readings on the spectographs they confirmed that the mother and child *tended to vocalise naturally in a coordinated and rhythmic way*. Spectrographs are not good at revealing high resolution fundamental frequency information, especially at lower frequencies. Quality can only be measured by pitch-plots and an interpretation of such a pitch-plot would allow those analysing the interaction to notice how *mother and infant match and alter the pitch and timbre of their vocalisations*. The perceived height of sound changing over time reveals what is called the melody. The final ingredient and goal is the narrative.

Much of this is very technical but put in simple terms we know that when mothers speak to their babies they use a distinctive sing-song manner of voice, and the baby listens attentively and with pleasure. There are examples of the babies showing such positive responses that the adult is impelled to 'sing' again or elaborate on her previous utterance.

Malloch *et al.* (1997) say that research on mother–infant communication, in which micro-analyses have been made of the behaviours involved, and experimental studies done of infants' reactions to different elements of human expression, has revealed that infants possess complex endowments for perceiving and stimulating maternal communicative signals. Infants can discriminate timing patterns, pitch, loudness, harmonic interval and voice quality.

These abilities emerge prenatally. It has been found that an infant learns its mother's voice from before birth, and after birth can recognise melodies or poetic verses played to her when in utero. Reactions of newborns to the human voice and their imitations of facial expressions, vocalisations and hand movements prove that this awareness of human signals, while slow and rudimentary, is both comprehensive and coherent at birth.

Think about this

Intimate connectedness

Malloch carried out some complementary research into mothers' expressions when they are talking/singing to their infants, which confirmed that both have innate systems that give them special abilities for sharing the meaning of life. Can you guess what these might be?

The speech of the mother to her baby has unconscious or intuitive forms that reveal the same characteristics in all languages. These forms include the tone or quality of a mother's voice and its rhythms and melody, which are all regulated in predictable ways. Malloch shows that these features match the demonstrated preferences that young infants seek in a human partner:

> *Typically, mothers everywhere repeat short, evenly spaced words with simple, sing-song intonations in a resonant yet relaxed and 'breathy' moderately high-pitched voice. Baby and mother listen to one another's sounds, creating co-operative patterns of vocalisations.*

(1999: 31)

What matters is that, from birth, the human infant together with the primary caregiver is able to establish a social collaboration based on how they express their feelings by adapting expressive movement, gesture and the sounds of their languages and culture. This allows them to establish what Gratier and Trevarthen (2008) call *intimate connectedness*. The early interactions of mother and baby allow the two to build a way of knowing one another within their own world, their own culture. For the infant language, the meanings of words or 'semantics', can play little part in this. She does, of course, hear the sounds and words of the language used by the mother, and she recognises rhythms and tones, but it is through the combined synchronous activity of gestures, vocalisations, expressions and feelings that she begins to contribute to and share and understand the knowledge and values of her culture. This intimate connectedness places her within her social and cultural group before she can talk. Gratier and Trevarthen (2008) propose that in the first six months of the infant's life, what they call proto–habitus is developed. This needs explanation. It was the French philosopher Pierre Bourdieu who defined habitus as a set of dispositions, habits or attitudes that explain the differences we see in all societies between and within groups. It is acquired by individuals and by groups through experience and is the product of the history of the family or group and of their particular class and cultural contexts. The prefix 'proto' means early or first. Gratier and Trevarthen (2008) say that '*habitus is nonverbally grounded embodied cultural knowledge that is expressed in practice by people connected through time within real communities*' (137). In other words, habitus is what groups of people do and know and value within their culture through sharing meaning. Habitus generally refers to communities of people living together. Proto–habitus is concerned with much smaller units within communities like that of the mother/infant dyad, their sharing with other members of the family, and their recognition by neighbours who know them. The simplest way of describing proto–habitus is making sense of and in a shared world.

Think about this

A very moving example of this earliest sharing is of a two month premature baby (32 weeks' gestational age) vocalising with her father. What do you learn from this?

> *The father is kangarooing his baby – holding her inside his shirt. The baby makes clear and simple calls which her father imitates. Both of them pitch their sound at about middle C. During the episode they exchange coos and both are spacing the vocalisations into phrase-like units of about four seconds, imitating one another. When the father does not respond, the infant makes three sounds, the first one rather weak but developing intensity and volume, calling him until he does respond.*

Malloch, whom you will remember knows a great deal about music, carried out a spectrographic analysis of the dialogue and found the father and baby vocalised keeping a regular rhythm at near 0.7 seconds between sounds, which corresponds to a slow or *andante* pulse in music (1999: 37). They maintained this until the father came in late for the last turn. Each interval equals a spoken syllable and a group of four of these corresponds to a phrase of speech. There was a lengthening of the last syllable. Malloch (1999) said this parallels the structure of spoken narrative in many details. And the pattern of sounds corresponds to the bars in music composed by the voice of the mother above middle C. In mothers who are depressed the voice is pitched at about an octave lower.

We know that we are born with an inner sense of time and in our earliest days show our feelings through the ways in which we are able to match our movements and sounds to those of the primary caregiver. So we are born being both expressive – able to reveal our feelings – and receptive – able to know the feelings of others. But researchers have observed that not all babies are always able to do this. Researchers noted that babies will show confusion or disappointment if, for example, the parent is depressed. Through perturbation tests they were able to note this when they filmed what happened when the mother was asked to be briefly inexpressive.

Universal or culture-specific?

When one reads what theorists state about what they observe in their society it is tempting to assume that their findings apply universally – to all people in all places. Yet, with regard to communicative musicality, researchers have found that there is cultural variation in the ways in which mothers and infants form bonds and interact in the early months of life. Face-to-face interactions are not encouraged in all cultures and communities and there are places where much communication with babies takes place through tactile and <u>kinaesthetic</u> modes of felt movement rather than the verbal, visual and gestural ones we see in protoconversation. And not all primary caregivers are mothers. There are differences in terms of timing and expression in the ways in which mothers and others reveal and share emotions and vitality in their exchanges with young children.

Powers and Trevarthen (2009) showed that the vowels of Japanese mothers talking with their infants vary more in terms of duration and pitch than the vowels of Scottish mothers. You will appreciate that the sounds of the languages of the world are all different. Mandarin, for example, is a highly inflected language, which means that it is a language that changes the form or ending of some words when the way in which they are used in sentences changes. This is not true of English. Yet both Mandarin- and English-speaking mothers adapt the rhythms and tone of voice and pacing of words to the patterns of motherese.

There are songs and rhymes, games and chants, in all cultures and plenty of evidence that babies everywhere are sung to. Most of the songs they hear come from the old histories of their own cultures – the chants and songs of their grandparents, passed on from one generation to the next. I remember my grandfather singing to me '*one potato, two potato, three potato, four* … (pause) … *five potato, six potato, seven potato more*', an originally Irish song, sung to me by my Russian grandfather in my South African home. The 'more' was my invitation to join in so the song was repeated.

Baby songs are made up of simple melodies, repeated motifs, and they often include simple accompanying actions. Groups of words, each lasting only for about 15 to 30 seconds, form the core element of these baby songs – a four-line stanza that has a beat or pulse which is at a relaxed walking pace – or in musical terminology *andante*. There are simple shifts of pitch and usually rhyming syllables at significant points and, in the last two lines, the beat might get faster or slower. A lullaby will be slower and a dance song faster. They are described as being narrative in their structure so they build to a climax, which then resolves. But mothers also sing their own versions of current popular songs, make up hand movements, bounce the babies to the rhythms – all aimed at drawing the baby into sharing the enjoyable enterprise.

The significance of music in our lives

There is evidence that music was an essential part of life for early human beings before language evolved, and throughout most of the 'developed' and the 'developing' worlds music still plays a huge part in our lives. Oliver Sacks, the famous neurologist and author was passionate about music and in his book *Musicophilia; Tales of Music and the Brain* he wrote about it and its impact on our lives and our feelings. He reminded us that music reproduces all the emotions we can feel but remains completely abstract. It is unique in the arts in remaining wholly abstract but still able to express pain and joy, sorrow and grief, love and jealousy and more. And he examined the very nature of music paying attention to the fact that, in music, repetition is essential.

> *There are, of course, inherent tendencies to repetition in music itself. Our poetry, our ballads, our songs are full of repetition; nursery rhymes and the little chants and songs we use to teach young children have choruses and refrains. We are attracted to repetition, even as adults; we want the stimulus and the reward again and again, and in music we get it.*

> (2007: 59)

He also said that we tend to impose a rhythm even when there is just a series of identical or similar sounds at constant intervals. '*We tend to hear the sound of a digital clock, for example, as "tick-tock, tick-tock" – even though it is actually "tick tick, tick tick".*' Enjoyment, performance and study of music has played a vital role in the lives of both Trevarthen and Malloch and both believe that it does much to promote social cohesion in all human groups. In some communities and with certain age groups music is integral to daily life.

Coda

In the two chapters you have just read we have been looking into the earliest exchanges between mother and infant and it seems only proper to end this with the words of Trevarthen himself.

> *One of the first things that people notice with an alert newborn baby is that they are extremely sensitive to the presence of another person, and especially somebody very close. They attend obviously to the voice, they look intently at your face, even though their vision is still not working very well, they orient towards looking at a person.*
>
> *We have an absolutely amazing film of a two month premature baby having a dialogue with the father, and the baby is inside the father's shirt, and they are exchanging coos, and the father is imitating the baby. And we looked at that very carefully and we found it had exactly the same timing as the syllables of speech, and that they are working on the same rhythm. And they seem to be sharing a sense of phrasing as well.*
>
> *So we have evidence from even a few minutes recording, that there is an amazing amount of preparation for human communication by rhythms and expressions of body movement, including vocalisation and face expressions. And recently there is a lot of interest in hands; because when we do films of newborn babies hand movement we find that they gesture, and make wonderful patterned hand movements which are not at all random.*
>
> *Young babies are very expressive, and the development is very fast, and so by a couple of months, six weeks of age, a baby's vision is clearly much, much more*

effective, and they look directly at your eyes, and the mother gets a very strong impression that a real person is looking at them, and then they can get involved in quite elaborate dialogues, conversations, but using very simple sounds and expressions.

I downloaded this from a website that has now been removed by Education Scotland. This is sad because seeing him and hearing him is often more powerful than reading about him.

Sharing minds

Intersubjectivity in the earliest months

In this chapter we consider how the human infant reveals her innate awareness of the feelings of others and starts to purposefully become a member of her culture.

We have seen how, in the earliest days or hours, the infant looks at and listens to the mother, searching for signs of what the mother is feeling. So far we have been following the vocal but non-verbal exchanges between the two, paying attention to the child and less attention to the eagerness of the primary caregiver to engage with the neonate. Trevarthen talks of the mother's drive to enter into dialogue with the infant as being what he calls '*intuitive parenting*'. It is this positive intuitive parenting together with the desire of the infant to communicate that fosters the aptitude for cultural learning that will lead on to language learning and many other invented skills.

This need of the infant for communication with a significant other is what allows for the understanding of self, and of self-with-other. We can think of intuitive parenting as what parents almost automatically and universally do to protect, feed, stimulate and induct babies into their culture. As you now know they do this through using motherese when they talk. The pitch and tone of voice of the mother catches the attention of the baby and draws her into responding to sounds or gestures, and then, if the mother falls silent or still, provoking responses from her. The role of the mother in her intuitive parenting is to start or maintain early protoconversations to enable the baby to regulate her emotional state and her impulses to do and know. Margaret Donaldson (1978), whose work you may well have encountered says,

> *Human sense is the understanding of how to live in the human and physical worlds that children normally develop in the first few years of life. It is learned spontaneously in the course of the direct encounters with these worlds that arise daily and unavoidably everywhere, transcending cultural differences. … The learning is continually informed and guided by emotion – that is, by feelings of significance, of value, of what matters. And it is highly stable and enduring, once established. It is the foundation on which all that follows must build.*
>
> (Donaldson 1978, cited in Trevarthen 2011: 79)

I have quoted Donaldson's work in the books I have written before, seeing her contribution to our understanding as being invaluable, but only when I began to read the work of Trevarthen did I fully understand what she was saying. Formerly I focused on the message it carried for teachers and early childhood practitioners, which was to ensure that what young children were being asked to do in nurseries and settings needed to make human sense to them. In other words, they could see the purpose of the task. I had completely ignored the aspect of emotions in this. *What children are involved in must matter to them.* We know that once young children enter settings where they are in group care they are often asked, invited or required to do things that are very abstract and removed from the discoveries of the child's daily life. They are often asked to do ridiculous things like colour all the big balls blue and all the small balls red or draw a line between the things that are the same. Such tasks, which have little meaning in everyday life, cannot matter to the child.

In search of a better understanding

The human infant is born into a society in which there are places, things and people. The social world is different from that of objects. Objects have no feelings and cannot relate to people or predict what they will do. Human beings, on the other hand, understand people on an intimate or on a more remote basis and know how to act together with others in order to do something together or achieve a goal, which may be shared. They can talk about what they do, and often have to predict what others will do.

 Think about this

Read through the description below of 15 seconds of 'dialogue' between a mother and baby boy of 2 days old, recorded by Emese Nagy in a Hungarian hospital that Trevarthen presented at a conference. It is a series of images/ slides of the baby accompanied by Trevarthen's comments as he showed the slides to an audience.

- In the first frame the mother has her hand in front of the baby's face with the index finger pointing upwards. The baby is focusing intently on the mother's hand as she puts up one finger. Trevarthen suggests the baby is asking '*Oh! Whose hand is that?*'
- In the second frame the finger is down and the baby is still watching closely. Trevarthen suggests that the baby is asking: '*What does she want?*'
- In the third frame the mother is not lifting her finger. Perhaps the baby thinks '*Oh well …*'
- In the fourth frame the baby thinks '*Better try to do that too*' (**and his heart speeds up**).

- In the fifth frame the baby moves a finger and thinks '*Is that right? I wonder if I can ask her to do it for me again.*' He looks at the mother's eyes (**and his heart slows down**).
- In the final frame the mother puts up the finger in response to his provocation and the baby thinks '*That's right. Thank you!*' (based on Trevarthen 2015: 15, Loch Lomond Symposium on *Action Anticipation*).

It is difficult to 'read' this without the images but you will have worked out from Trevarthen's commentary what it is the baby might be thinking as he watches the mother.

Can you see how the baby, after imitating, not getting a response from the mother, copies her action again in order to invite or provoke a response? According to Trevarthen the infant would need to understand, or feel, what the other person might be thinking about or intending to do. So an infant would need to sense that another person moving can think and feel and have intentions like her own. In order for the infant to be able to communicate she needs to be able to adjust her thinking and feelings to what she assumes to be the thinking and feelings of the other person.

The work of Nagy and Molnar (2004) to determine whether newborn infants merely copied what adults did in front of them or whether they actually initiated actions for others to copy is conclusive here. They called the observed behaviours of the newborn babies who made an action requiring a response from another <u>provocations</u> – i.e. provoking a response. And that is exactly what we saw with the baby in our example above – raising one finger in response to the mother doing it and then repeating the action to provoke a response from the mother. They found that neonates were not only able to imitate but were also able to initiate tongue protrusion gestures apparently seeking a response from the adult. They also found that imitation and initiation of tongue protrusion showed different heart rate patterns, suggesting that they may be served by different <u>psychophysiological</u> mechanisms. It seems that 'provocation' actions are anticipated by heart rate getting slower or decelerating whilst heart rate increases before and during an imitation response. Now isn't that fascinating? I am a very sceptical person and need to have something scientific to back up assertions made. And here we have it. You will now appreciate why, in the *Think about this* section above, the heart rate pattern is mentioned.

Coming to understand the world involves the processes of subjectivity and intersubjectivity. Subjectivity means making a judgement based on individual personal impressions of the self, feelings and opinions rather than on external facts. You might make a subjective decision about whether you like the art of a particular painter or choose to read the novels of a certain author. Intersubjectivity is defined as '*existing between conscious minds; shared by more than one conscious mind*' (Oxford Dictionaries 2010). So subjective behaviour requires a recognition that others have thoughts and feelings like the self, and also, for Trevarthen, the ability to show, by coordinated acts, that purposes are being consciously regulated. This means that the infant adjusts her actions or gestures or expressions in order to achieve something, to carry out a plan. The baby cited copying holding up one finger shows the baby watching, thinking, predicting and making changes to achieve a desired goal – in this case for the mother to copy what the baby has done. It implies that infants are able to relate objects and situations to themselves and predict outcomes through the expressions, actions and gestures they make. What is happening with infants engaging in these tiny dialogues with the mother is that they also reveal their awareness of another person with another mind who also has plans. This is intersubjectivity.

Belonging to a family and a culture

It will not surprise you to learn that a few decades ago it was thought that the human infant was, at first, totally dependent on the mother or primary caregiver for care of bodily needs, and only this. As Trevarthen says 'like a "patient"'. In the scientific or medical literature of the 1950s there was no suggestion that the infant was also, and crucially, consciously engaging with others and that this behaviour was purposive. As has been mentioned, one paediatrician working to help babies have a good experience of birth changed this. Berry Brazelton greeted newborns in a gentle friendly way, and they attended to him and watched how he moved something he was holding. They showed intelligent interest and pleasure. Brazelton shared this observation with the mother and father, and they were delighted. That is what they were waiting for, a new playful member of their family. Trevarthen, in his work with Brazelton and Bruner, wanted to discover more about the newborn person and now many of those working with young children and families are happy to believe that the human infant is purposeful and sympathetic, wanting to be a member of her family and with her community and culture.

The new understanding came out of close and in-depth analysis of film clips of newborns and older babies with their mothers and/or fathers. Trevarthen noted that when the baby is rested and alert and in the company of those who are clearly sympathetic to her, the actions and gestures and vocalisations she makes invite intensely positive responses from the mother or father, and perhaps brother or sister. The consequence is that the baby's companion has an immediate sense of interacting with her as a little human person who is a curious learner.

Each of these interactions takes place within a context – a world that is not only physical but also cultural. Every baby is born into some culture, a traditional community with its language, customs, beliefs, rituals, history, artefacts and more. The mother vocalises; the baby listens and hears and vocalises back. In response the mother will say something in the language of the culture. In English she often may say something like, 'Oh really! Well tell me some more then.' The baby listens, hears and vocalises back. These are the protoconversations we have talked about earlier in the book. Moreover, Trevarthen argues that the human infant is interested in deliberately expanding this knowledge in the companionship of others and, over time, as she engages with others not only in protoconversations but also in sharing objects, songs, games and rituals – all of which may be particular to her culture – she gains a sense of pride in belonging to that family and that culture. You will find more about this in Section 2.

Barbara Rogoff, working with groups, many in central America, was very interested in how, in these cultures, babies were almost always with other people of all ages, and part of whatever they were doing. If, for example, the adults were cooking, the baby might be given some pastry to pound and roll and play with; if the women were weaving, the babies might be given coloured threads. In one of her books there is a photograph of a very small child holding a machete as he walks into the woods with his father. You can imagine how that shocked readers in the developed world!

These babies and small children were watching and being part of the daily tasks and celebrations specific to their culture. Rogoff called this <u>guided participation</u>, and Trevarthen calls it <u>collaborative learning</u>. The baby is engaged with another or others in sharing meaning – all with intense participation.

 Think about this

In Trevarthen's talk on *Why Attachment Matters in Sharing Meaning* (2009a), the audience was shown some of his wonderful and illustrative film clips, and two of these are very revealing.

- In one the baby was sitting on her mother's knee with a book to look at while the mother opened and read the telephone bill with great interest. The baby dropped her book on the floor and pointed to the telephone bill making an urgent, enquiring sound. So the mother put her down and gave her the telephone bill. She took it eagerly and studied it with a great deal of attention while she sat on the floor.

Why, do you think, was the baby more interested in the bill than in her picture book? Trevarthen suggests that it must be because the mother was so intently interested in it. Perhaps the baby was wanting to know why that particular object was of such interest to her mother.

- In the second film clip a Japanese mother and her little boy aged ten months are together as the mother sings a baby song, making many hand gestures to tell a story. The little boy watches her like a critical audience or 'judge', and, at the end of the mother's performance makes the traditional and polite bow to her.

Do you think that he is not only sharing the meaning but also exploring the rituals and practices of his culture, judging how well his mother shows him the familiar story? The film clip reveals just how conscious he is of his achievement. It is clearly important to get such things right.

It is significant that both these children are past nine months of age – the little girl being one year old and the Japanese boy aged ten months. That is the age around which children in all cultures and all kinds of families gain a new interest in what special things other people, whom they know well, are doing, with attention to what they choose to do with them. One mother made a telephone bill important; the other became an actress playing her part in action songs her baby knew. The significance of this development will become clearer in Section 2.

An appraisal of classical attachment theory

You may have come across the work of John Bowlby. He was a doctor who developed what became known as *Attachment Theory*. Studying primarily babies and toddlers, whom he had observed becoming distressed when separated from their parents – often as the result of being kept apart in hospital – he examined the intensely close bond of emotions between the infant and mother. He saw that it was so strong and binding and essential to the baby's well-being that when that mother was no longer present the baby experienced a deep sense of loss, or grief. He placed a great deal of emphasis on the baby's need for mother as a special person rather than on the act of mothering or care-taking.

Trevarthen accepts that the mothering role, the one played most often by mothers, is special because of its very intimacy and response to vital needs, but he reminds us that, even for newborns, fathers and grandparents, siblings and friends – anyone who can engage in intimate and repeated dialogues and have fun – can become important to the child. This kind of companionship will help the infant communicate and enjoy social interactions. Bowlby suggested that children come into the world biologically pre-programmed to form loving attachments with others for support and care. Trevarthen tells us that children also come into the world being innately sociable, which means that they are keen to build meaning through shared narratives, interests and projects created between them and the people they love. The ways in which the infant turns to people and imprints (or copies) what she observes from her carers' actions, gestures and feelings are what will help her survive and enjoy it. This is a biological theory about how the human infant develops relationships at two different levels. Trevarthen's view is more social and cultural. Here is an extract from the transcript of a talk he made on the subject of attachment:

Well the child has a very, very strong instinct to find other people, because they are the only thing in the world that can confirm belonging and the need to be part of a community. They have to be in community with people, so they can form a private world. We all have an attachment to the house we live in, or the room we sleep in, or the objects that we possess, and babies can be like that too, but really they can't have companionship with an object, it's limited, very limited, and they know that. Winnicott talked about having a blanket as a substitute for the mother; it's not, because you can't have a conversation with a blanket really. You can have a conversation with yourself, using the blanket to support the idea, but that's not quite the same.

So babies are looking for companionship, they are looking for somebody. And I would like to make the point that the baby's looking, or curiosity is more important than any parent's desire to teach the baby, or anybody's desire to teach the baby; the baby is not a pupil, it is not just an ignorant human being that needs to be taught knowledge. To be part of a human community which is sharing knowledge and understanding you don't have to have a teacher, you just have to have company, good company, and that company can be of any age. And that is something that I would like to emphasise, that certainly by the time the baby is three or four months old siblings, older siblings can be very good companions, and play with the child happily. And I think that by the time the baby is six months old they can get along fine with a group of other kids of different ages, they don't have to be all the same age, and they don't have to be all babies, and they don't have to have adult supervision all the time.

(educationscotland 2016)

The early interactions we have been talking about – the protoconversations – are not serving the survival of the baby as an organism. They are different from the shared routines and actions like nappy changing, breast-feeding, stroking, rocking and other behaviours aimed at easing some problem of the body. When acting in order to engage playfully in a communicative exchange about interests and discoveries in moving and sensing the baby has shown no sign of need or distress. The interactions are enjoyable and calm or well-measured, depending on sequences of looks and utterances accompanied by vocalising and touching, using hand gesture and facial expression to make signs. Baby and parent communicate in a short series of sustained movements with shared attention and a rhythmic pulse. They appear to be engrossing and enjoyable for both partners in the play, satisfying a need to feel good together. Measuring changes in the neonate's heartbeat as in response to novel events or objects, for example, can also be used to show that the infant is sensitive to expression of emotions of her carers, through their tone of voice, change of expression and body movements. A clear example of this was cited earlier in the film clip of the neonate's heart beat changing in response to what was happening in a dialogue of imitations studied by Nagy and Molnar (2004). All of this serves the formation of a strong attachment between baby and primary caregiver.

Summing up this section

We have looked at the extraordinary development of the human infant from the moment of conception to shortly after birth and seen how everything the newborn child does in her earliest interactions with significant others is directed by the baby, assisted by her primary caregiver, at becoming part of the social, intellectual, physical and cultural worlds she inhabits. Trevarthen's thinking, and that of those who influenced his research and collaborated with him, makes us view the infant with new respect. This is no helpless creature but a human being using everything at her disposal in her complex body with many senses intentionally to connect with others in order to get to know what they know in order to make and share meaning.

Section 2

The remainder of the first year of life

Since all babies develop differently, my decision to divide the book into sections showing development according to age is merely a device. Some children will do things earlier than others, some later but that has little or no relevance for their development. They will all grow and change.

In this section we continue from where we left off, with our neonates and two month olds interacting with primary caregivers, engaging in the beginnings of protoconversations and communicative musicality, and knowing that others have thoughts and feelings. You will find as we watch the newborn travel through the rest of her first year of life that important ways of acting and reacting remain in control of how the child practises being alive, gaining new skills and awareness. We chart her progress through playing person-to-person games, recognising her image in the mirror, reaching and catching, being able to visually track moving objects, imitate actions like pointing and clapping, to playing with objects and sharing what they mean. At around six months she is already an able and self-conscious performer. At around 40 weeks or nine months we see her reaching a pivotal moment as she begins to cooperate with others in shared tasks and moves from protoconversation to protolanguage.

Chapter 2.1

Towards secondary intersubjectivity

In this chapter we look at how changes in the baby's body and mind provoke changes in the ways in which the mother or other primary caregiver responds.

As the infant becomes older there are evident changes in her size, how perceptive she is, her motor strength and her ability to coordinate her movements to achieve her goals. She develops the ability to pay attention for longer, to differentiate between things and to collaborate with others in her social and emotional interactions. She learns new habits and enjoys a familiar world.

Developmental diaries

Tracking a newborn's development by keeping a developmental diary has been done famously by many people, including Charles Darwin. When my first grandchild was born, nearly 21 years ago, I had just become interested in how babies develop and I kept a developmental diary of her progress for the first six months of her life. When my own children were babies I was too tired and anxious to do anything more than love and care for them. You might be amused by my observations and perhaps notice that my focus was on the baby as being totally dependent on others rather than purposeful in her social and emotional engagements. A very unTrevarthian analysis!

 Think about this

Think about what this developmental diary says about how thinking has changed in 21 years.

6 weeks: smiles at her mum and holds up her head.
7.5 weeks: looks at faces, plants, paintings; turns in the direction of mum's voice; pushes down with her feet; lots of mouth and tongue movements; watches my mouth as I sing.

9.5 weeks: real social smiles; lots of pseudodialogue; a range of cries; smiles at and talks to my earrings shaped like birds and a jumper with patterns on; can hold her bottle.

10.5 weeks: range of sounds – shriek, gurgle etc.; studies her feet; responds to finger clicking, hand clapping; listens to singing and makes sounds when it stops; turn taking.

11.5 weeks: joins in when her mother sings along to music; can entertain herself for 20 minutes – just looking.

12.5 weeks: her mother says 'A milestone!' By accident she hit the ball attached to a mobile. Then repeated the action and kept on doing it – sometimes smiling, sometimes crying. Intentional behaviour?

3 months: Playing peek-a-boo, she predicted and began to look over the top of the cover; watched the film 'Singing in the Rain' and cried when it was turned off; likes singing, clapping games, photographs of people; shows an intense interest in books.

4 months: really looks in the mirror and grins at herself: beams with anticipation when her mother starts 'The owl and pussy cat went to sea ...'. If you count '1, 2, 3 ...' she waits with baited breath for what is coming next; holds and examines objects. Her mother said 'She has learned that changing the shape of her mouth affects the sounds she makes. I can hear her practising her vowel sounds'.

Even from these small extracts it is evident that my analysis of what I was seeing and hearing was rooted in what we might call classical child development theories. Can you see that I was only charting what the baby was doing and paying little if any attention to the consequent changes in the responses, reactions, initiations and provocations of the mother? Although I noticed important things like Hannah's interest in people and in music and her attempts to join in, this is still an incomplete portrait because there is no appreciation that what she is doing at all points is purposefully trying to become part of her particular world and its people. There is no recognition that what she is doing is both making and sharing meaning.

Note: At that time the word protoconversation was unknown to me so I invented my own word 'pseudodialogue', which suggests fake dialogue rather than first dialogue.

Periods of rapid change

Trevarthen and Aitken (2001, 2003) tell us that infants not only grow bigger physically and develop their muscle strength and coordination in order to achieve goals they have set but, also, as a consequence of developments in their brain, become able to refine their abilities of discrimination and their social skills so they become able to interact and cooperate with others. They respond to the emotional signals they get from those caring for them. In the course of the steady development of memory, motives, interests and personality, there are rapid changes in the growth processes in the brain related to 'epigenetic' events, which result in what is called *periods of rapid change* (PRCs). These apply primarily to will and curiosity. The significance is that each rapid change in the baby's behaviour makes particular demands on the responses of their parents or carers.

In my developmental diary, when Hannah was only about four months old, I recorded this: 'I reckon she is a genius because she looked from an image of Matisse cut-outs in a book to a Matisse print hanging on the wall'.

It is clear that I found this a startling thing to have happened and thought carefully about what she would have learned in order to be able to do this. The Matisse print had been hanging on the wall of the sitting room throughout her life. It was large and colourful and she often looked at it with interest. It was familiar to her and in her memory – in her present and also in her past. I had brought a book with examples of Matisse cut-outs for her to look at because the colours and shapes were so bold and colourful. Something about the small cut-outs must have reminded her of the familiar painting on the wall. Her responses showed that she had been able to remember, compare and evaluate. She had seen two things that were similar and tried to check that she was correct.

Trevarthen says that the infant begins to keep track of events and relationships in her life with her growing memory. Researchers like Donaldson (1978) have carried out tests using controlled displays of sounds or sights and observed that the baby's memory gradually but steadily improves.

 ### Think about this

Think about how the baby at around 40 weeks begins to react to strangers, showing wariness and even fear. Is there evidence of the baby at this stage displaying intense anxiety when the mother or primary caregiver is not present or when an object she seeks is hidden or missing? What does that tell us about memory?

Ainsworth *et al.* (1978) tell us that it implies that the baby must have a memory of the person or object that is missing and an awareness that a stranger is not someone she remembers. As a result the baby begins to display the emotions of fear and anxiety but, also, at the same time, a sense of playfulness – or for play with meanings. Donaldson (1992) says that the change noticed at this stage is the start of what she calls the *line mode* of consciousness and she explains this as the child being able to remember a past, live in the present and imagine a future. It is the start of a '*story time*' that will be filled by known places, activities, objects and people. The child can also make comparisons and appreciate resemblances (Carey & Xu 2001) and, as Reddy (2003) says, join in jokes involving the strange behaviour of others, especially familiar others, which can be imitated.

Trevarthen and Aitken (2001) describe this as a journey from primary intersubjectivity to person–person games to person–person–object games and manipulative play, to showing off and fear of strangers, and then to secondary intersubjectivity.

Person–person or person–person–object games

During the second half of the first year of life the intentions of the baby towards people and objects change. Richards (1980) tells us that at four months of age the baby begins to change her intent focus on the eyes of other people, choosing to look with interest instead at where she, the baby, is and what is within her reach. Around the age of six months, however, her interest in people is resumed with greater intensity of emotion, evidenced by making more eye-contact and smiling or frowning. The adults, responding to and provoking the reactions of the infants, join them in play with objects. When three people are involved in the play it is called triadic play. Murray (2014) offers the example of Astrid, aged four and a half months, involved in a tickling game with her mother, whilst her father looks on. She reveals her awareness of his presence by looking to see what he is showing on his face and clearly seeks to engage him in the process.

Play and games are part of relationships in all cultures and part of the ways in which children learn how to communicate with others about themselves and to share ideas as meaningful. The interactions are playful and how the infant responds to the games and jokes, the tricks and magic will determine, to a large extent, how her consciousness of her particular identity – her personality – develops. Games have rules and by companions drawing the baby into regulated changes of intention and emotion, she is being prepared to accept the joint interests and purposes necessary for the game to work as something with valued meaning. The baby comes to know that interests must be joint and that to alter aspects of the game requires cooperation. Bråten (1998) says that '*At this age infants in familiar company show "prestance" or self-other consciousness and pride in ritualized performances*'. He says that when the infant is with an unfamiliar person in such a game she may experience anxiety and mistrust (18). It was Trevarthen who, in discussion of infant play, introduced the term 'prestance', which he took from the French philosopher Wallon and his definition of it is slightly extended from Bråten's. He agrees that it means that the baby develops a presence or a self to present to others. And the baby delights in this and will show off or perform to any available and friendly audience. Conversely if the baby's performance does not capture the interest of her audience she will feel shame rather than pride. He emphasises that pride and shame are 'basic complex emotions' with fundamental 'moral' value in our development and learning with others.

When the baby is about nine months or 40 weeks old there is a significant leap in understanding. Murray (2014) calls this a shift to more connected-up understanding. She describes this as the period where *'babies start to join up their different skills and experiences in new ways, also showing a growing awareness of other people's take on the world and of how this connects with their own experience'* (21). They are combining their interest in the world, their ability to communicate with others and their knowledge of others' experience of the world. Murray illustrates this with a classic example: Ben, aged 10 months is being fed by his mother when he spots his tractor on a shelf. He shapes his hand and fingers into a pointing gesture and waves it in the direction of the tractor. Then, significantly, he turns to his mother and pulls his features into a look of pleading. He has joined up his desire for the tractor with his finding a gesture to indicate this desire and knowing what facial expression to use to impel his mother to address his need.

The infant now shows a new awareness of the importance of cooperation. She imitates what another is doing and this is taken as an indication that she can share attention, share goals, work together to achieve a goal. Babies and their partners use vocalisation and gesture or pointing to share, follow and direct interest with the other. When, for example, the mother changes the direction of her eyes the baby follows her gaze; when the mother looks pleased the baby repeats what it is she has done. When the mother suggests something the baby follows her signals. This is what Trevarthen originally called *secondary inter-subjectivity* where the baby's increased curiosity about what people are doing and how and why they are using certain objects to do it lead the baby towards learning language.

 Think about this

Trevarthen offers two film clips to illustrate this. In the first, Emma, just 7 months old, when asked to put the toy man in the toy truck chews the man and stares at the truck rather than complying with the request. In the second, Basilie, aged 12 months, completes the task with ease, following the mother's indications.

Also, at around this time, the infant does not simply respond to the emotions of others or join in with or resist their invitations to play or explore objects. Let's look at an example of a baby and her mother with an object. The baby pays great attention to her mother, trying to work out not only what her mother is doing with the object but also what her mother wants her to do with the object. She implicitly questions also whether her mother likes or dislikes what she is doing, and so on. Here is an example showing the development of Ben, whom you met earlier in this chapter, revealing his ability to communicate, give and share, join in and cooperate, drawn from Murray (2014: 23).

> *Two months later Ben's mother plays a hiding game with him. He is sitting opposite her at a table and she has hidden her face from him behind a cloth. He watches intently until she removes it whilst saying 'Boo!' The mother smiles and Ben looks at the cloth, reaches for it and tries to cover his face with it. His mother responds with an anticipatory sound of 'Aaaah …' and when he removes the cloth is rewarded with 'Boo!'*

Sharing behaviours and symbolic potential

Now, as the infant begins to show evidence of being aware of how she and the things she does are understood by others, she becomes more involved with studying and making meaning of the behaviours and feelings of others. Imitation of the gestures of others, their mannerisms and vocalisations and ways of handling objects become almost routine and the baby begins to combine sounds and movements into what Trevarthen, following Michael Halliday's explanation of the development of his son Nigel's mastery of language, calls '*acts of meaning*'. This is how the baby – not yet using spoken language – can yet both give and receive messages. In other words this is how the baby becomes capable of using sharing behaviours.

Objects and actions, through play, attain *symbolic potential* for the baby. Halliday called it 'learning how to mean'. They can come to stand for or become something else. For example, a simple rubber ball can roll, but it can also bounce and it can be chewed and, if thrown at something, might break it or hurt someone. It can be large or small and come in a range of colours. Actions involving the rubber ball can evoke different responses and feelings. The ball being held by the child might be wanted by the mother; it might make a scary noise when dropped on the floor; it might ease your gums when being chewed. Trevarthen reminds us that the ball, as an object, in examples like the above, is in the awareness of at least two people. That is what makes it a symbol that can be given a name.

To help us understand more clearly, we need to look at the work of Lev Vygotsky (1978) and consider the words *intramental* and *intermental,* which he used to explain his ideas. You will know that the prefix 'intra' means 'within' and the prefix 'inter' means 'between'. Vygotsky said that intramental ability exists within the child while intermental ability occurs in the relationship between people. Remember that Vygotsky was operating within a belief system that the human infant was not capable of purposive or intentional behaviour for many months to come. For Trevarthem however, when the purposive baby is engaged with another person and an object, the object is in the minds of both. It can exist as an object but also be represented in some way by a symbol, perhaps a picture or a written or spoken word. It is important to add that, although Vygotsky did not conceive of the human infant being purposive, he did understand how, from birth, babies are inducted into the social and cultural worlds in an 'intermental zone of proximal development', by the support of older persons. This zone of proximal development is the notional gap between what a child can do alone and what that same child could do with help. Educationalists will be familiar with this term, which is often used to highlight the essential role more experienced learners play in supporting the learning of less experienced children. It was the work of Vygotsky that first drew attention to the natural engagement of infants into the worlds of their families that led the way for us to understand that the human infant is programmed for social and cultural development.

After three months, as the baby becomes stronger, more curious, eager to look at surroundings, and to grasp and manipulate an object she is attracted to, person–person games begin, and in these games the baby is often the performer, showing off her skills. Then she starts exploring with her hands, and her person–person games are elaborated by the addition of objects or toys. Now there develops in the baby a developing tension between doing something for herself, or with others – and this makes for increasing self-consciousness, teasing and fun and invention of games. This is why the infant begins to find mirrors interesting at this age – they tease expectations of communication.

Babies engaged in person–person–object play are not only coming to understand the minds and meanings of others but also aspects of their own culture. The objects that are used in this play will vary from culture to culture. Rogoff (1990) has pictures of babies using rolling pins with dough copying their mothers' cooking; in Zanzibar I saw babies playing with stones, handing them to an adult who handed them back. Anything familiar and available can be used to make up a task. When I was working in South Africa I encountered a baby and mother using seed pods as shakers; another parent using torn rubber shoes as a bed for a doll; an older brother offering an off-cut of wood as a car. In each case the object used held symbolic potential for the child, and in each case the object can be considered as a cultural tool.

There is little space in this book to examine the literature around the interactions of babies with books. In these exchanges the infant with one or both carers, alone, or with peers, is being inducted into new worlds – real, imagined, in images and words, with pages to be turned, a front and back, top and bottom. They are cultural tools to be explored and shared.

On the next page there is a photograph of Hannah at nine months of age intently watching her father turning the pages of a flap book.

 Think about this

Who do you think initiates communication sequences involving infant, caregiver and sometimes an object? The mother or the baby? Hubley and Trevarthen (1979) noticed that it was primarily the mothers who initiated these exchanges when the babies concerned were between nine and ten months of age but after that it was the babies who chose new topics. And it was the infants who largely chose to stop an interaction when they had had enough. Read this extract from Rogoff (1990: 80), which shows how adults and babies manage attention during exchanges. In the example cited the baby is six months old.

> *The adult began by trying to get the baby's attention, calling the baby's name in a loud and friendly manner as he shifted his face back and forth in front of the baby and leaned into the baby's line of gaze. The baby avoided the adult's line of gaze, and sat gazing fixedly into space to one side, where there was nothing obvious to attract his attention. ... The adult stopped calling the baby's name and trying to move into the baby's line of gaze and, instead, looked over toward whatever the baby was looking at and asked softly, 'What are you looking at?' ... Immediately after the adult's shift to share the baby's focus of attention, the baby sat up, looked directly at the adult, and smiled, ready to interact. ... Then the adult turned back to meet the baby's inviting gaze and the interaction continued with pleasure.*

In another extract from the book there is an example of a baby of ten months old playing with an adult looking at a tower of rings. The adult made signs, tapping the tower, and the baby watched intently and imitated the actions. Over a series of moves the baby was proudly able to push one ring off the tower. In her analysis of this sequence, Rogoff tells us that the baby seemed able to interpret the adult's intentions and what she calls the '*game script*' and this required the baby to examine the many cues given by the adult through gaze, expression and timing. And the game ended when the baby decided it should.

So the baby and mother have moved on in one year from primary intersubjectivity – the tiny episodes of protoconversations in face-to-face mirroring exchanges to secondary intersubjectivity. At around 40 weeks they show that, with another person and attending to the use of an object, they are able to make sense of what they can do, what others can do, what objects are for and what they can do together in collaboration. They are able to share attention and their moves are referential, signalling ideas beyond the bounds of the present situation. They can think back and ahead; remember and imagine. They try to capture the attention of others and measure to what extent others are paying them attention and following the plot.

Socioemotional development

In this chapter we examine how, during this first year of life, the infant not only develops a sense of self and others as agents with intentions and awareness, but also a sensitivity for complex emotions – her own and those of others.

Developing an awareness of self and of others: of the expected and unexpected

We have looked at attachment earlier in this book and we know that in the first few months the infant has established an intense and intimate attachment with the mother through interactions characterised by increased playfulness of body movements and sounds. The baby is becoming more demonstrative of her feelings, and ready to share them in the person–person and person–person–object games that involve other family members – the father, siblings, grandparents and others. Games like 'round and round the garden', with a song or rhyme, some physical actions that help tell the story and often a dramatic and satisfying climax, become family rituals, repeated over and over again. Over time the baby begins to play a more active role in initiating, responding to and altering the play.

Gratier (2003) and Gratier and Trevarthen (2008) suggest that a '*proto-habitus*', or early appreciation and enjoyment of particular performances as rituals, develops through the first few months, and the baby learns and perfects her own particular performance, offered to get the approval and appreciation of her audience. In doing this she will draw on what she has seen and heard, all of which are shaped by the culture of her home and community. In order for her to do this she has to have developed her innate sense of herself and a sense of others. Panksepp and Northoff (2009) describe the self–other awareness demonstrated through these early performances as being anoetic, meaning a pure experience of feelings or expression of emotion, in the body without specifying any object or cause. In summary, the baby has moved on from enjoyment of the ritual forms of early games to being eager and able to adapt to the particular ways of expressing feelings in her culture. She has become eager to perform to others and she displays self-consciousness as self-other awareness of what is being done. It is important that this development of meaning grows from an anoetic emotional consciousness of self and other and does not demand her having a *theory of mind*, as some theorists would suggest.

Those accepting the idea of theory of mind believed that preschool children only became able to know the feelings and thoughts of others when no longer babies or toddlers. Trevarthen, as you now well know, demonstrates that even very young babies are aware of other people's thoughts and wants and have no need of a 'theory' of their own mind or that others have minds. Others think that this form of rational understanding is required, and that it does not develop until the toddler or preschool years after the child is speaking. This contradiction can be resolved by taking a developmental view, understanding how communication of states of mind grows from an innate ability to 'sympathise' with others' actions – that is, how early-developing intuitive awareness of their intentions and feelings later becomes more reflective and explicit or 'talked about'. Trevarthen offers the case of a six-month-old baby performing the actions of a known song to receive praise and applause with pride, and the same infant responding with confusion and anxiety to a stranger who does not respond to the child's performance.

By seven months the baby begins to demonstrate more vigorous and rapid rhythmic movements, which may include banging with the hands, and also syllabic babbling, which Darwin (1871) suggested might be the innate repetitive motor function that makes the learning of speech possible. It is around this time that the infant, seeking intimate communication, begins to show a more intense awareness of the quality of response from a partner. If the response of someone the baby knows is blank or negative, the infant displays wariness and distress. Similarly an infant who wants intimate communication will show wary attention and withdrawal if approached too directly by a stranger who 'does not know the game' as practised in play with family (Trevarthen 2005; Reddy 2008).

This increased sensitivity to the actions, emotions and needs of others takes place just before the striking change that takes place at nine months as shown in the infant's willingness to share a task that requires particular actions on or with objects in cooperative work (Trevarthen & Hubley 1978; Hubley & Trevarthen 1979). Cooperation requires synchrony of actions or joint activity with a common sense of time. Throughout early development, indeed from before birth, a matching <u>hierarchical</u> set of rhythms of movement helps in the coordination of motives and actions between infant and adult. There has been a body of research into what causes the infant to display signs of anxiety and perturbation tests, for example where the baby encounters a blank or still face – one that shows no emotion – the baby is sensitive to both the affective quality of a parent's expressions and to their contingent timing (Murray & Trevarthen 1985). We know too that the spontaneous movements of the infant demonstrate self-synchrony between body parts, and in communication the baby and parent show precise <u>intersynchrony,</u> which means matching movements and gestures to be as one.

Between the second and fourth months of life, as the baby gains more experience she becomes used to face-to-face interactions with parents, grandparents, siblings, strangers and others. She has learned to recognise them and expects to play with them and to find these encounters positive. So the number of people with whom the infant can interact and begin to share meaning has enlarged from the parents to include more family members, friends, neighbours and other adults and children encountered in daily life. In this way the baby encounters increasing numbers of people not yet known to her – that is, strangers.

There is experimental evidence that babies are unhappy when something unexpected happens to confuse a dialogue, as Trevarthen expresses it. Perhaps the mother is feeling ill or sad and becomes more silent and more unresponsive than usual. When this happens the baby's response is to show distress by crying or withdrawing her attention. Murray (2014) tells us that when the mother or other partner turns away for a different reason – without showing negative emotions – the baby merely notices what is happening but shows no distress. Whilst the baby is practising these reactions she is also becoming better attuned to the particular way in which her mother and/or father engage with her. In other words she is working out the particular style of interaction used by them. If the primary carer, for example, is regularly very responsive to her then the baby will prefer interactions with other people who are very responsive. The baby is developing what we might call social sensitivity.

 Think about this

Murray (2014), in her engaging and very easy to read book, tells us of Ben, aged 17 months, sitting on the floor with a bowl of snacks in front of him when he catches sight of his reflection in the oven door. He points to it as an object of interest. He begins to perform, watching intently what his image is doing. He puts one hand on his head and takes a long, hard look and then he tries to take off his bib, still watching himself in the oven door and then moves the bib around. His father is watching this and offers him a hat that he often likes to put on. Ben puts on the hat and is so entranced by what he sees in the mirror that he shrieks with joy.

Contrast that with the example of Iris, who, at 14 months old was taken to a research laboratory where her interactions with her image were assessed using what is known as the *rouge test*. This involved her mother putting a dot of rouge on Iris's nose in a room with a large mirror on the wall. Iris sees her image in the mirror, crawls over to it, stands up and kisses her image. She looks at her image, but appears to not recognise it as her image and so looks for another baby behind the mirror and then loses interest. Four months later the rouge test is repeated and this time Iris recognises herself in the mirror – red nose and all.

This is significant in showing that the baby is becoming aware of her self on her journey to come to know about herself in relation to others. She lives in a world with other people – a social world – and it is through their companionship that she will make meaning.

 Think about this

Trevarthen (2005) has written a paper called 'Stepping Away from the Mirror: Pride and Shame in Adventures of Companionship': Reflections on the Nature and Emotional Needs of Infant Intersubjectivity'. Can you highlight or underline or just make a note of the words or phrases in that wonderful title that tell you what it might be about? For me all the words here are important but my initial thoughts focus on the significance of the words in the main title. The meaning of the subtitle is apparent.

- *Stepping away from the mirror* means beginning to know that there is a self and others and also that moving away from the self is an important thing to be able to do. Trevarthen says it is a metaphor for the mind of the infant starting to take the initiative when in the company of others.
- *Pride and shame* refers to what happens when the baby begins to perform for or join in with others and how sometimes she feels pride and sometimes, when she does not achieve her goals, shame. Remember we are talking of a baby only a few months old.
- *Adventures of companionship* make me think of how the infant seeks the company of others for playful or risky play and exploration.

It is often the baby who takes the initiative in interaction and it is important to know that each interaction involves thinking and feeling. Meaning is made and shared in a collaborative and what I am calling *playful protofriendship*. Trevarthen explains it like this: '*Infants are born with a bold self-consciousness of this kind: one that soon takes responsibility for independent acting and thinking, but that also may feel pleasure and pride in the approval of others, and shame at failure before them*' (2005: 56).

It is around the middle of this first year of life that babies show an increasing social awareness. They join in, laugh, show off, demand attention, become playful – all of which actions and behaviours are designed to seek a response from others – particularly appreciation and recognition. They are truly social in their behaviours, seeking company, companionship and collaboration. But if the child encounters someone who does not respond to her advances or responds negatively she will withdraw and feel rejected and shamed.

In some of his work Trevarthen says that he is not particularly interested in 'cognition' or knowing and reasoning, but is trying to understand what is called 'conation', the striving or urge to do things that make experience. He thinks this effort is the creator of learning and intelligence. Most importantly, the shapes of action that make intentions and satisfy interests are appreciated by other people. We have seen that from birth the child is learning and her learning depends on the opportunities for her to share her impulsive acts with someone familiar – usually a close family member. The baby chooses to share her acts with someone who reveals an equal eagerness to share with the baby. It is a duet – two active partners, both committed to the discovery or revelation of things to be learned through playful joint activities. Accompanying the spontaneous interactions between baby and parent are powerful emotions and motives: it is an ongoing sharing of experience that last a lifetime.

 Think about this

Trevarthen offers the delightful example of three-month-old Laura, who is shown engaging with three family members all playing separate but interlinked roles. The mother is engaging in protoconversations with the baby; the three-year-old sister tries to join in the game whilst the father looks on with pride. No one is consciously teaching or testing the child. It is part of the everyday sharing of meaning in a family group.

My question is this: do you think it possible that the baby is educating the adults and her sister in how to discover and share meanings that make sense and bring pleasure to them all?

As the baby develops a repertoire of actions and responses to and with her partners, she refines her understanding both of herself and of others. She imitates and replies to their actions, makes her own gestures and vocalisations to make her meaning clear. She is partner and performer, actor and audience.

Until relatively recently it had been believed that it was only at the end of the first year of life that a baby becomes aware of the self–other dichotomy but Reddy (2003) showed that this happens far earlier. At around two months of age we have seen how the infant responds to attention given to her by someone else. A baby will smile when her mother makes eye contact with her and stop smiling when the attention directed at her is removed. By about four months the baby will actively and intentionally try to attract attention from someone else by making sounds that Reddy calls '*calling vocalisations*'. A few months later the baby will engage with others by showing off or performing with the aim of getting attention that has not been given or has been withdrawn. Or the baby might repeat an action or sound that attracted a positive response. Young babies are often seen to repeat something that has made someone else laugh and these infants begin to tease others by acting in silly or surprising ways. Reddy says the importance of this is that it shows that *the infant, by the end of the first year of life, is aware that she has the power to command the attention of others.* What she does affects what others do.

By about seven or eight months, as has been mentioned, the baby tends to develop both a stronger attachment to the mother or other primary caregiver and, at the same time an awareness of strangers, whom she may regard with wariness. Having welcomed each newcomer with smiles and attention, the baby at this stage becomes aware that someone new to her might pose some threat.

In terms of social and emotional development the concept of attachment, the love of someone special, mentioned earlier in the book, is important. Babies develop bonds with people from birth and the bonds they form with their primary caregivers – those with whom they have the closest emotional and physical ties, who support and protect and engage with them – are known as attachment bonds. These are different from the ties they have with other people they encounter in their lives. Attachment relationships will be formed primarily with parents and close family members – perhaps with grandparents and siblings, for example. They will be few in number, but as the baby gets older she will form strong bonds of special friendship with a limited number of people other than those in her family.

Adaptations of the human body and brain

We have been thinking of how the child in this first year of life becomes aware of herself as being distinct from others and very interested in them. For intimate communication, the baby is born with many special body parts and special senses for sharing life with other persons. Trevarthen (2005) tells us that humans are unique amongst primates in having a white *sclera* in the eye and it is this that makes it possible for them to notice small changes in the direction of gaze of others. Monkeys and apes have dark scleras. The white of our eyes helps us to know how the person whose gaze we are tracking is feeling or thinking. Inattention to what another's eyes are signalling is said to be one symptom of autism or abnormal 'self-absorption' in a child. Trevarthen states that:

> Only humans have this monitoring of momentary shifts of gaze, which serves an intersubjectivity, face to face, capable of detecting shifts of thought and feeling even when they indicate experience of events of another time and place and with arbitrary meaning.

(2005: 66)

People who are blind pick up cues about how others are feeling from touch or the sounds of their movements or from the change of direction and expression in the human voice. So a blind child will compensate using her other senses. Human hands, too, are uniquely adapted in their shape and mobility so that they are able to indicate intentions and feelings in delicate ways from birth.

I want to cite again the wonderful example of a film clip made by Gunilla Preisler (1986) in Stockholm, of a blind baby girl, aged five months old, showing what she does in response to her mother singing her familiar songs. The little girl, never having seen her own hands or, indeed, any hand is yet able use her hands to accompany the songs she hears to both express her own feelings and to respond to the feelings she receives from the sounds of her mother's voice. She 'conducts' her mother's melody like a professional conductor, moving her finger up for a rise in pitch, gracefully tracing a phrase and closing a verse with a downward movement of her palm, Sometimes her hand moves a third of a second ahead of the mother's voice. She knows the song as a feeling of moving in her body, and improvises an accompaniment to her mother's singing voice, following its poetry.

Coming to understand feelings

Emotion is such an everyday word that we all know what we mean when we use it or read it or hear it. But do we all mean the same things when we use or encounter the word? In my search for an acceptable definition I found several. Here are a few to think about:

   Emotion means …

- *an affective state of consciousness in which joy, sorrow, fear, hate, or the like, is experienced, as distinguished from cognitive and volitional states of consciousness.*
- *any of the feelings of joy, sorrow, fear, hate, love, etc.*
- *any strong agitation of the feelings actuated by experiencing love, hate, fear, etc. and usually accompanied by certain physiological changes, as increased heartbeat or respiration, and often overt manifestation, as crying or shaking.*
- *something that causes such a reaction* (from www.dictionary.com).

Trevarthen (1993) says that many people over many years denied that it was appropriate to talk about young babies having emotions on the basis of them not yet having a self-concept and enough experience of social scripts. Some theorists have even claimed that the baby only develops emotions after having witnessed the emotion displayed to them by their primary caregiver.

   It was Daniel Stern's work that opened our eyes to the significance of *affects*. The word *affects* is quite difficult to define but generally has two meanings: the first being to have an effect on or make a difference to something, to change it; and the second to touch the feelings of someone, or move them emotionally. Stern talked about dynamic or *vitality affects* and affect attunement, and he followed the developing ability of the infant to engage in coordinated attention with another. At first, sharing of affections is in a social, person–person experience – the dyadic state when the very young infant enjoys brief protoconversations with the mother. This moves on to triadic person–person–object projects where the baby's curiosity about the world is influenced by the degree to which mothers are affectively attuned to what the baby is interested in at that moment. So the ability to take part in what the other person is experiencing subjectively, understanding their thoughts and what they intend to do, depends on sharing their feelings, sympathetically. In this way affect attunement is the basis for the first meaningful communication of thinking and, as Stern (1985) puts it, most importantly, provides a way for mutual appreciation of the other's mental state.

Trevarthen (1993) asserts that there is clear evidence that the infant is born with what he calls a coherent and differentiated emotional system, which, he says, '*covers, in miniature, the full range observed in adults*' (73). He compares this miniature range of emotions to the tiny hand of a foetus or neonate, which has five tiny fingers. With this delicate hand and the rich variety of self-related feelings, the human infant has the essential 'equipment' necessary for expressing and sharing emotions. The hand moves fingers and gestures to indicate interest or to comfort the body; the infant brain is equipped to generate all the emotions necessary for successful social interaction. He goes on to say that in his analysis of changes in the communications between mother and baby over this first year of life it is impossible to deny that the baby experiences and displays emotion. Initially the emotions may be related to an encounter with a person, an object or something happening within the infant's own body. Some neonatal facial expressions, gestures and vocalisations are adapted to elicit parental care – for example a need to sleep, to be fed, to have another blanket and more. Others, such as smiles, reaching out to touch and seductive coos, express more playful needs, which transmit emotions of pleasure or interest. These emotional messages regulate learning in company.

 Think about this

We have established that socially important meaning is shared before the child acquires language, through playful collaborative interactions with caring others, and it is clear that the infant is seeking to find pleasure in engaging with someone who is or will be responsive. So *the role of the other in the early interactions is key*. What the infant is seeking to do is to find her place in what Trevarthen (2005) calls a community of 'common sense' or meaning-making. Read now what he says about how investigations of what happens in the brain show that the

> mechanisms which coordinate and guide intentional and investigative movements, infuse actions with emotion, evaluate goals and discoveries aesthetically in the regulation of learning and that signal all these motivating events to others – show that deep seated emotional systems have a role in both the sharing of emotions and experiences with others and adaptive change in the growing brain and its cognitive capacities.

(2005: 55)

We are all born with a brain prepared for these activities, and ready to develop them. Even before the baby can stand or walk she has refined her awareness of other people and their feelings. She has done this through her intense episodes of intersubjectivity. The infant can express complex emotions and is ready, from birth, to share her feelings with the feelings of others. The effects of this on the child's intellectual ability are dramatic and profoundly important for the early development of perception, motor coordination and cognitive processes. To a degree unequalled in any other primate, the human baby starts to learn by communicating. Think about this. It is an extraordinary idea. Trevarthen explains that all later developments show that *the regulation of learning by emotion in communication is of primary importance for the whole strategy of human mental growth*. I place that sentence in italics because it is so important to our understanding. The foundations for communication by emotional expression are innate as is the course of their development. New reasons and opportunities for communication emerge in an age-predictable progression as new goals for learning are set.

It is important to consider carefully the significance of the caregiver's role in interactions and I offer you the fact that Charles Darwin, writing as long ago as 1877 and who, as you know, kept developmental diaries of his children, concluded from the record of his son when he was only four and a half months old: '*An infant understands to a certain extent, and as I believe at a very early period, the feelings of those who tend him, by the expression of their features*' (1877: 294).

 Think about this

In a 2016 episode of *The Life Scientific* on BBC Radio 4, Frans de Waal talked about our close affinity to the chimpanzee and particularly the bonobo apes. It was, of course, Darwin who first alerted us to the importance of our ape ancestry. Modern genome analysis tells us we share 99 per cent of our DNA with our closest relatives in the animal kingdom – namely the chimpanzee and the bonobo. We have tended to think of apes being fierce and territorial and we may be surprised to learn that, on the other hand, they are kind and clever, traits we tend to like to think of as being uniquely human. De Waal is a behavioural biologist and best-selling author and has spent many years observing the behaviour of chimps on a daily basis. He pioneered studies of kindness and peace-making in primates, when other scientists were focusing on violence, greed and aggression. Empathy, the recognition of another's feelings, he argues, has a long evolutionary history and de Waal is determined to undermine our arrogant assumptions of human superiority. Perhaps we are closer to our ancestors than we previously believed, since there is now a growing body of clear evidence that they share many of our emotions.

So what does this suggest to you about how important the role of caregiver is for the infant becoming able to recognise, share and respond to the emotions of that caregiver? Trevarthen (2005) tells us that human behaviour is different from that of monkeys or apes in that it reveals a more developed capacity for reflective thinking, which is the ability to reconstruct or remember things that have happened in order to construct imagined future events and to make narratives about them. To do this the human being must be ready to learn many new skills, and to plan ahead and imagine things perhaps never experienced to a degree that is beyond other species. The human infant, through looking, listening, imitating, feeling and thinking about what the caregivers are themselves doing, thinking and feeling is also attending to the reactions of the caregiver to the actions and reactions of the infant. They are creating and exploring a treasure trove of experiences together.

How infants strive to know their culture

In this chapter we explore how, through the companionship of others, the baby begins to learn her culture and her language.

We are all born into a culture that may be defined according to the language or languages we speak, the religions we follow or reject, the music and literature and paintings and dances that we learn to perform and enjoy, the foods we eat, the tools and utensils we use, our attitudes to other people and cultures, and the rituals and ceremonies and performances we engage in, and so on. We define our culture according to what matters most to us. From the very moment of birth – perhaps from conception – aspects of our culture have an influence on who we become. You know that Trevarthen's thesis is that the human infant is intent on becoming a member of her group – her family and her culture – and she does this through the myriad interactions – tiny and large – that take place initially with her mother or primary caregiver and then with other family members and friends. In this chapter we examine this theory in more detail.

It will not surprise you to learn that Trevarthen, with his scientific background and deep understanding of animal behaviour and brain science or neurophysiology, brings a fresh view of just how the human infant comes to not only join others within a culture, but to interact with these others in deliberate ways by which the older and/or more experienced others are inspired to teach her. He calls this a theory of *innate cognition for social and cultural skills* (Trevarthen 1988: 37). Recent research in this field tells us that human infants are born with a self-regulating strategy for getting knowledge through negotiation with others and in cooperative action. Children learn social behaviours and language itself in a 'zone of proximal development' where their attempts to know the world are supported by the responses that more experienced or older people make. So socialisation or cultural learning is as natural, as innate for the human brain as is walking, feeling, seeing and breathing with human limbs and senses.

Educational theorists, including Jerome Bruner, writing about slightly older children talk of adults 'scaffolding' children's learning where the scaffold is the support given to what the child wants to do. In such a situation a child might

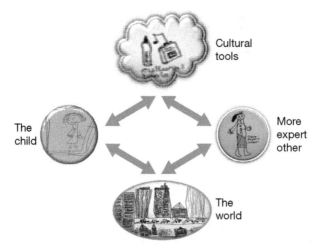

Figure 2.3.1 Child with more expert other using text or other cultural tools to mediate experience. It is what enables the child alone to use cultural tools to mediate experience.

be building a tower of blocks and reaches a point where she clearly needs help. The parent or teacher might offer physical support to the child or suggest that she might come up with her own plan for what she might do next.

Trevarthen, observing children from their first year of life before they are using language, finds that they are being 'taught' new awareness and skills through interacting or 'conversing' to compose narratives of action or play games with more experienced others. This is very close to the views of Lev Vygotsky (1978) who said that the child learns about the world through the support of a more expert other using cultural tools. The word he uses for what takes place during the interaction is mediation. The diagram above comes from my book *Introducing Vygotsky* and shows the child and mother using an object or cultural tool to make meaning of her culture.

Ostensive marking

Part of the role of the mother, father or other companion includes being able to assist the baby in understanding the goals or intentions of other persons when they are drawn into an exchange relating to objects or events. Here is an example of just such an interaction offered by Murray (2014).

 Think about this

Isabel, aged nine months, and her mother are together in the kitchen. As you read this try to work out just what it is that the mother does to draw Isabel into understanding something she might not have experienced before. You are looking to see what the mother does to help Isabel become part of a cultural act taking place in her home. In other words, look out for what the mother notices about the baby and how she responds with what Murray (2014) calls ostensive marking and explains that such ostensive marking consists of signals given by movements such as raising her eyebrows, smiling, gasping, holding her breath and making spoken comments.

- Isabel is sitting in her high chair chewing on a rusk while her mother is peeling a melon to include in a drink she is preparing for her child. Looking at Isabel she lifts up the piece of melon to show her, explaining what she is doing.
- She shows Isabel the peeled melon.
- She cuts the melon into small pieces, all the while talking about what she is doing. Isabel watches and listens attentively.
- She lifts up a slice of melon and offers it to Isabel to try.
- She hands the piece of melon and the baby explores what it feels like.
- Now the mother shows the baby that she is going to put a cup under the spout of the juicing machine.
- As she moves to press the button which will start the juicing process she signals with gestures and facial expressions that this is going to be the really exciting part.
- As the machine whirrs away and juice starts to pour into the cup the mother smiles and shows her delight.
- Finally she pours the juice from the cup into Isabel's bottle (Murray 2014: 29).

I noted that the mother looked at the baby and at the objects being used; she showed the baby the melon; talked – giving explanations and reasons for action; checked that the child was looking and listening; actively involved the child, drawing her into the activity; demonstrated; changed her facial expressions and smiled in conclusion.

The significance of Relatedness

It was initially puzzling for me to find the word *relatedness* being used by Trevarthen and others in describing the early interactions between baby and mother, but when I found that in addition to it meaning a connection by kinship, common origin or marriage, when used in connection with music it means to have a close harmonic connection. This makes perfect sense when we think of the bond of activity that is formed between the infant and mother and how important it is that this is a secure and two-way bond. It also makes sense in light of Trevarthen's expressed interest in the role of music in our lives. Murray (2014) says that *connected-up Relatedness* (and yes, she does spell relatedness with a capital R) develops the baby's understanding of other people and the role of social interaction. According to Murray this significant shift in social development, to a more 'connected-up relatedness' (2014: 27), involves the infant developing a greater sense of other people's experiences in the world and how these experiences relate to the infant's own experiences, which is essential to 'mature social understanding' (25). Although signs to a more 'connected-up' social understanding include infant reciprocity with others, following instructions and drawing others' attention to something by pointing, how infants reach this stage may not yet be entirely known (Murray 2014).

Between four to six months the baby will take notice of objects that are close by, easily visible and in a place where she can follow what is happening by changing the direction of her gaze. By the end of the first year she can follow the gaze of another person and that enables her to look for, or imagine, things that may not be in her direct line of vision. At around the same time the baby's gaze will dart ahead in anticipation of what someone might be going to do and will also show surprise and interest when the gaze of someone moves from one thing to another. Murray suggests that it is now that the infant can distinguish between events that are deliberate and those that are accidental.

Initially most early interactions involve two people – mother and baby, but many babies will soon enter three-way interactions, usually mother, baby and father. Murray has an example of a triadic game of peek-a-boo between Saavan who is six and a half months old, and whilst he is sitting on his mother's lap his father is appearing and disappearing, much to his delight. In the photograph we see Hannah engaging in examining a book together with her mother and a friend's daughter.

Universal cooperative motives

One online dictionary defines cooperative motives as *the ambition or temperamental propensity to react in an adjoined manner in sociocultural and behavioural environments by assisting other people in attaining their own objectives* (*Psychology Dictionary* 2017).

My definition is actively joining in with others who share the same goals or intentions. In his chapter on universal cooperative motives in Jahoda and Lewis, Trevarthen (1988) compares communication between mothers and infants in Scotland and the United States with that of mothers and infants in Lagos, Nigeria. His samples in the developed world consist of dyads whom he describes as being primarily white and western. He is looking to see if the ways in which the mother interacts with the baby alter the patterns of the development of communication. In essence he is looking at different cultural and familial styles of interaction and then at how they affect the development of communication between mother and child, trying to discover the natural motives of the child and of parents, mainly mothers, that coordinate and guide the development of cooperative awareness and learning of conventions in infancy.

This is a summary of what we know about the findings on communicative development in Scotland and parts of the United States.

- Immediately after birth the infant pays attention to human faces and voices.
- She demonstrates that she can make different facial expressions and respond to the tone of voice of the person she is interacting with.
- The mother is generally attuned to the needs and feelings of her baby and can detect and appreciate the action, vocalisations, expressions and gestures.
- The infant, in turn, is sensitive to the contingent actions, gestures, expressions and vocalisations of the mother.
- At about 40 weeks the baby becomes more alert and eager to interact, look, listen and join in when the mothers is showing ways of using objects.
- The mother speaks to the baby using repetitive baby talk or motherese, which changes as the baby's expressive behaviours develop.
- After the first month the mother and infant join in face-to-face proto-conversational interactions, which are characterised by vocalisations that become regular and modulated so that there is a sequence of evenly spaced utterances that are synchronised with the movements of head and face.
- In this primary intersubjectivity we see a communicative duet between mother and child where each must adapt to the actions and utterances of the other.
- There is a growing strengthening of the bond established at birth between mother and baby, and between three and five months of age the baby demonstrates a new interest in where she is, whom she is with and what they are doing.

- In the second half of the first year of life the baby imitates playful expressions, shows increasing awareness of self and other and takes over from being teased to teasing others.
- When engaging in person–person–object games the baby shows awareness of the feelings and intentions of others and is able to not only communicate in ways that select particular goals, but also to collaborate in shared tasks and meaning-making. This prepares for attention to words of language and speaking to name objects or actions.

In Lagos, with the help of Alistair Mundy-Castle, Professor of Psychology at Lagos University, babies and mothers were observed in a specially constructed TV recording room at the large and busy teaching hospital in a poor but very lively community in Idi Araba of Lagos (Trevarthen 1988). They were also studied by a Yoruba-speaking graduate of Professor Mundy-Castle's department who visited them at home, made detailed descriptions of play with the babies, took videos and asked questions of the mothers. A rich collection of photographs of the everyday life of the babies was made by Trevarthen's young colleagues Penelope and John Hubley. There were 21 subjects, 12 female and 9 male, recorded between 3 and 52 weeks old.

It is important to note that observing intimate private play to make assessments of what was seen and heard was more complicated than in Edinburgh, because family life in the Yoruba community, and the role of mothers and fathers, were expressive of very different cultures.

The main findings in Lagos were as follows:

- The interactions showed the key developments through the first year of playfulness and cooperative awareness and learning were as in Edinburgh, but the mothers' responses were more what Trevarthen calls coercive. Social life in Lagos is vigorous and demanding. There is little privacy.
- In the recording room of a crowded hospital there were many distractions and the mothers expected to be told what to do. While loving and attentive, they were more instructive and provocative with the babies than the mothers in Scotland, often showing impatience when the babies were unresponsive or fretful. They were used to living in one room about 12 feet by 12 feet where they slept with their children, ate their meals and relaxed. Several of these rooms opened onto a compound in which families mingled, and from soon after birth babies interacted with familiar people of all ages. The mothers worked in the neighbourhood, busily earning their living, selling fish or prepared food, sewing, cooking food. Often their infants accompanied them, even as one-year-olds, carried in a cloth wrapped round their bodies that supported them on the mother's back, where they could share the mother's work, even, in one case, chopping firewood with a large axe. Fathers lived a separate life and were often absent.

- The mothers were judged to be controlling and reluctant to give control to the babies. Mothers in Edinburgh were more softly spoken and following the baby's lead.
- Babies of only one month old watched the movements of the mother, rarely smiled at her and then only in response to sounds or touch. They were more responsive when alone with the mother in the home room.
- They made expressive movements of the mouth and hand gestures, to which the mothers responded with lively touching of face, mouth or hands, bouncing the baby's body and singing with a slow rhythm. They used pulsing touches and jiggled the babies' cheeks to stimulate smiles.
- The mothers looked regularly at the babies, and when they were asked to sit quietly with a still face looking at the baby, one-month-olds became restless, waving their arms and vocalising with grimaces. Three- to five-month-olds stared at them then looked away to explore the room; or they become vocal and moved their arms about. They did not become distressed. When the mother spoke again, they immediately smiled.
- One newborn imitated tongue protrusion. She stared at her mother's tongue, then opened her lips and moved her tongue in clear imitation.
- As with the Edinburgh infants, play became more joking and teasing in the fifth month, when the infants developed the ability to grasp objects. Lagos mothers were more active and directing in play than those in Edinburgh and their infants were more attentive to their performances. They were not so helpful in presenting the ball on the string, frequently keeping it out of reach of the infants and swinging it quickly about to play with them. The infants joined in games with squeals, yodeling and growling noises, which the mothers imitated. They also watched their mother's hand move, and some tried to imitate hand clapping.
- Between six and nine months the Lagos infants became more vocal, more vigorous in reaching for the ball and more playful with it, laughing and squealing when unable to catch it, intensely interested in manipulating and matching the wooden dolls with the truck and greatly amused by teasing games with the mother, learning to repeat performances. They began to attend to her instructions with the truck. When the mother kept her face still and remained silent, the older Lagos infants became vocal and tended to 'show off'. These behaviours were essentially the same as those observed with the Edinburgh subjects, but the Lagos infants were more active, used to running about freely in the compound by one year, and very unwilling to sit in a chair for the photography.

Overall, although there were clear cultural differences in styles of parenting, the babies in Lagos were lively and expressive and, assisted by their lively mothers, showed the same developmental progress By one year they were cooperating with their mothers in games, imitating gestures and vocalisations and creating humorous actions to perform to the mother and others, advancing towards communication with their language, Yoruba. Strangers also became more of a threat when they were about nine months old and taking interest in their mothers' special habits and tasks.

If you can find a copy of this book do look at the photographs taken of the Lagos infants with their primary caregivers and companions. They give an interesting view of babies communicating in ways we immediately appreciate, although we have grown up in a very different community and culture.

Trevarthen acknowledges that little or no attention was paid to social class in this study and the damaging effects of poverty were not addressed. Recording effects of stress or illness was not the objective of the study, which was to increase understanding of the natural impulses of the healthy child and responsive parent to develop shared understanding. The families in Nigeria were poor and the mothers had to work hard to support them, but adults and children were healthy and generally happy.

We know that in many communities the impact of poverty on individuals and groups can be devastating. We have only to consider how babies currently born in Syria, for example, suffer life-changing emotional disorders and will fail to develop cooperative skills. Nevertheless, neglected and maltreated infants do develop, trying to fulfil the goals and needs for experience in relationships that are part of a growing human person, and with these powers they respond to therapies that sensitively support the enjoyment of communication.

 Think about this

The realities of poverty

As I write about development I am always aware of the fact that living and writing in the developed world, taking advantage of its rich resources, instruments of communication and means of mobility, leaves me in the position of possibly disregarding and failing to address the realities of the world I live in. It is 2017 and yet there are still babies being born into families that do not have the means to feed and sustain them. Here is a quotation from the work of two South African researchers, Kate Sherry and Catherine Draper (2013), which makes grim reading but is a much needed reminder.

> There is increasing evidence that the first 1000 days (pregnancy and the first two years of life) are believed to represent a window of opportunity for growth promotion (Victora, de Onis, Hallal, Blossner & Shrimpton 2010), which is especially relevant for children from deprived settings. Appropriate stimulation during the critical first two years will come primarily from parents or alternative caregivers, and the capacities and resources of parents therefore become highly significant. A growing body of evidence exists on the impact of maternal depression on early development, possibly through reduced mother–infant bonding, parental responsiveness and therefore early stimulation (Engle et al. 2007). Effects are not only cognitive: in a

cohort study carried out in the UK, a weak association was found between cognitive development and maternal depression, but a strong association between depression and behavioural problems, indicating difficulties with socio-emotional development (Kiernan & Mensah 2009). Common mental disorders, such as depression, are known to be strongly associated with poverty (Lund et al. 2010; Tomlinson 2010), heightening the risks for childhood development associated with poor socio-economic circumstances. At the same time, maternal education is also found to be strongly associated with early development (Engle et al. 2011; Handal et al. 2007) and is a further factor associated with socio-economic status.

It is very important to remember that poverty and its consequences are not limited to what economists call the developing world. We have a great deal of poverty in this country and there will be those reading this book who may themselves live in poverty and/or suffer from anxiety and depression. It is important to remember that all parents want to be good parents, to interact with their sensitive and clever babies who want to play and to establish strong bonds with them. All parents will do the best they can according to their circumstances. Diversity of opportunity is our reality.

A South African case study

I found this tiny case study of only two newborn babies, both born prematurely, in South Africa. I include it as an example of things that might be universal and things that are not. It refers to the work of Pascoe, Bissessur and Mayers (2016).

Mother and son: Abigail and Anat.

Abigail was an 18-year-old woman living in low-cost housing in Cape Town. After going for a routine check-up at the community clinic, she was diagnosed as suffering from a condition that might lead to renal dysfunction. Her baby boy Anathi was born in hospital after a Caesarean section at 33 weeks of gestation weighing only 2050g. Abigail is bilingual and her first language is isiXhosa. At the time she was living with her aunt, nephews and nieces in a two-roomed house and had started attending college. The plan was that after the baby's birth her aunt would look after Anathi during the day.

After birth, Anathi was placed in an open cot and fed infant formula orally through feeding tubes. Abigail was not able to have any physical contact with him for one week post-delivery while he underwent phototherapy and he was tube-fed during this initial period. Abigail started *Kangaroo Mother Care* (KMC) after one week, and you will remember that this is where a parent carries the baby inside their clothing in order to have skin to skin contact, which benefits the baby's development. She began cup and breastfeeding Anathi and his feeding tube was removed. She remained in the hospital with the baby until he was discharged, about ten days after birth. For some reason this meant that she was only able to hold and interact with him for three days prior to him leaving hospital.

We are told that Abigail felt unprepared for the baby's early birth and was scared by the medical difficulties he faced after birth and the implications of all of this for his development. She felt that she lacked information about the medical condition of her baby, and would have liked more information about the feeding tubes and the reason why she could not breastfeed till she started KMC. She would have liked to receive more support from the staff at the hospital but instead turned to her family to help her with breastfeeding.

You will almost certainly agree that this was not the best way in which the two could form a strong bond.

Mother and daughter: Beverly and Blair.

Beverly was a 33-year-old woman living in Cape Town, with her husband and two daughters. Her third daughter, Blair, was born at 33 weeks gestational age with a birth weight of 1900 g. Like Anathi, Blair was born in hospital because his mother had been hospitalised at 33 weeks due to a placental abruption – where the placenta partially or completely separates from the uterus before birth. The baby can be deprived of oxygen and nutrients and there may be severe bleeding in baby, mother or both. The hospital to which she was admitted was a private hospital and this is where an emergency Caesarean section delivery was performed. Beverly was a teacher and a monolingual English speaker. Her other daughters were aged three and six years old respectively.

Beverly was able to hold Blair shortly after birth, before she was admitted to the Neonatal Intensive Care Unit or NICU. Beverly stayed in the hospital for three days, whilst the baby, Blair, stayed in NICU until she was discharged, about three weeks after birth. So it was a long period of separation. During her stay in hospital, Blair underwent various procedures and tests including phototherapy for jaundice and being connected to a C-pap machine to assist with breathing for the first four days after birth. Afterwards, she was placed in an incubator for one day, before moving into an open cot. Again, like Anathi, Blair was fed through feeding tubes orally while she was on the C-pap machine, and nasally afterwards. A week before being discharged, she started being bottle fed and was thus able to leave hospital able to feed orally and with no need for any feeding intervention. Beverly and her husband were able to hold Blair once she was off the C-pap machine. After being discharged, Beverly would visit Blair at the hospital once or twice daily. She tried to practice Kangarooing the baby for about an hour every day from there onwards. After Blair was discharged from hospital, Beverly would still place her on her chest, but not necessarily practice skin-to-skin contact.

Beverly had been very shocked and upset when she found out that she needed an emergency delivery. She was also worried that Blair might have medical problems and reported feeling guilty for not being able to spend much time with Blair at the hospital, as she also needed to care for her other children at home. Blair exhibited some aversion to touch for the first few days after birth. She cried and became distressed when touched by anyone. Beverly felt that Blair's aversion to touch together with the complexities of holding a premature baby in an NICU made the bonding process for her and her husband difficult. She was not able to bond with Blair while she was in hospital as she spent considerable time sleeping. Beverly did report that Blair was more relaxed during Kangarooing and this helped them slowly start bonding.

Two mothers, two babies, two premature births, two disruptions to the beginnings of intimate contact and bonding. How will these babies' communication develop?

If you are able to read the whole article you can track the development of the baby as communicator with her mother through the comments of the mothers.

 Think about this

This was a tiny sample for a piece of research and the researchers had a specific brief. The authors of the piece are speech and language practitioners and so their focus was very much on the development of communication. The full article is rich in statements made by the mothers concerned. But here are their findings for you consider.

> There were huge differences in the economic, educational and life experience of these two mothers – one a teenager from a relatively low socioeconomic group and the other a woman already a mother, educated to tertiary level and living in an affluent part of the city. Both gave birth under fairly traumatic conditions where the babies were premature and mother and child could not form a bond immediately after birth. And yet both responded to the baby as well they could and the babies achieved the expected communication milestones in their first year of life.

The impact of maternal depression on infants

We have mentioned John Bowlby who, with René Spitz, was influenced in the 1930s by Sigmund Freud's psychoanalytic studies of mental illness. Together they made perhaps the first studies to make the link between psychoanalytical theories and biology. Like Trevarthen, Bowlby had knowledge of several disciplines and his well-informed interpretation of the emotional needs of infants revealed by their behaviour when they are separated from the person closest to them continues to inform our understanding, particularly of the mother–infant bond. The neuropsychological 'structure' that shapes the tie between babies and caregivers has been named the *attachment system*. This emotional and behavioural system was conceived as something innate and instinctual, a need rather like hunger and thirst. It is a system that organises the baby's memorisation processes, which make her strive to interact and communicate with the mother from the moment of birth.

Trevarthen, with a clinical colleague Kenneth Aitken (2001), identified a particular group of neurons that are genetically programmed and form what they called the 'intrinsic motive formation' (IMF). This leads the baby's brain to develop an <u>affective interaction</u> with the mother's care. The baby's attachment is said to be intersubjective and interpersonal, motivated to be expressive of, and responsive to, feelings of a body with the urge to move, and to move with another. As you know, the prefix 'inter' means 'between'. So the attachment has to be between the two selves. When the mother approaches the baby with sensitivity and responsiveness of love, a fine rhythmic organisation of synchronic or alternating responses is triggered between them.

It is clear that the attachment system increases the baby's chances of survival in the sense that when an immature brain addresses a mature one to fulfil its basic needs, the mother's brain will be moved to feed and nurture her baby. But *a strong bond is about more than that: it is essential to the well-being of the infant as a whole imaginative person and will affect her ability to make strong and positive bonds with others in her life.* In other words an adequate link between the mother and the baby is crucial for the development of a safe attachment system for the future, but the link must be fed by the baby's responsive behaviour. A safe attachment between the baby and the mother or other caregiver fosters the baby's well-being and her basic confidence and pride in future relationships, while an unsafe attachment is related to increased anxiety and persistent shame.

The importance of companionship

Trevarthen, in an article published by *Psychoanalytic Dialogues* in 2009, writes about the full significance of 'companionship' with others, children or adults, for the human infant (Trevarthen 2009b). He insists that the infant is born with motives to create consciousness of a rich, rewarding and productive life with others. I imagine that you don't really think about companionship in your everyday lives: it is something you have hopefully always had and take for granted. Trevarthen refers to the metaphor of sharing bread, which is the original meaning in Latin: '*com*', meaning 'with', and '*pain*', meaning 'bread'. Here is how he expresses this:

> bread is something people fabricate from a long cultivated part of nature that other people will consume to live, and, although it has been enjoyed for countless

generations, it tastes best when fresh made. The mind-nourishing 'bread' of culture is its meaning – the stories we share about 'what' happens, 'where' and 'when' it happened and 'who' were involved. It is full of sympathy and drama of human intention and desires. Being so valuable, meaning and belief in it is also fought over when in short supply and rejected when stale or moldy. Not all our efforts to share meaning are generous or nourishing.

(Trevarthen 2009b: 508)

He goes on to say that there has been little study of how humans come to know about the world together – in other words, to make meaning as human sense, through companionship. As we might expect in light of his training, he again turns to science of the brain. Charles Sherrington, who was one of the main influences on Colwyn's early studies of the nervous system, revealed how sympathetic movements of human bodies are driven by oscillations of energy in the human brain that generate prospective intelligence with proprioception, the feeling inside the body produced by its moving. This means that *human beings, like other animals, must act with anticipation of the consequences*, and that *they must be able to share the proprioceptions of their different bodies*. This is evident in person–person–object interactions where gestures, facial expression and vocalisation are imitated and enable us to communicate with the minds of others. We communicate about real and possible, anticipated and imagined events and this is alive in this first year of life. A baby watching her mother 'conduct' music she hears playing on the radio and joining in as a co-performer is an example. The baby is making sense in her self, in her body, of what it is the mother is responding to, what her body movements express and what she must be feeling.

 Think about this

According to Trevarthen there is an established body of evidence showing that the human brain is uniquely adapted for communication about states of mind and learning cultural routines or rituals that express feeling and movement. More recently it has been shown that the neural activity in every person's brain responds by revealing to another person with what he calls, '*an immediate living sympathy for the motives made evident in the actions of other persons, how they are seen or heard to direct their movements and control the experiences they stir up*' (2009b: 510).

In a study using functional brain imaging to locate activity of neurons in the cerebral cortex, Tzourio-Mazoyer and colleagues (2002) have shown that when a baby of only two months of age sees the face of another person who might be someone to communicate with – a prospective companion – areas of the cortex become active. What is amazing is that these are the same parts in the brain as those of a sophisticated adult being aware of the face expressions of another person.

The road to language

In this chapter we look at Trevarthen's ideas on how the human infant comes to understand and speak the language/s of her home and culture.

Some influences on Trevarthen's thinking

Trevarthen was interested in the work of Jurgen Habermas (1970) and Joanna Ryan (1974), both of whom considered the role of interpersonal awareness, which they called 'intersubjectivity', in the development of language. Both recognised the significance of the infant being able to make and share meanings with others, and Ryan said that children begin to speak by communicating feelings and interests with familiar people. She paid attention to *'how mothers succeed in questioning, prohibiting, informing, encouraging or rejecting the infants before the latter can speak'* (cited in Trevarthen 1988: 8) and believed that communicative competence (which is the ability to share purposes, ideas and feelings) is fundamental and comes before language.

Gratier and Trevarthen (2007) tell us that the mother and baby, from their earliest protoconversations, move

> to the same tempo and mutually regulate sympathetic human contact, with a deliberate 'courtesy' like the address and reply of an improvised and amiable debate. The parent often refers to the speechless infant 'saying' things, or 'telling a story'. Infants not only produce modulated vocal sounds but also produce them at the right moment within an ongoing flow of speech addressed to them.
>
> (2007: 171)

If you listen to mothers responding to their infants you can often hear comments like 'Oh, you think that is funny, do you?' or 'What a story you are telling!' (both overheard by Sandra Smidt on London buses).

It was Habermas who used the term 'intersubjectivity' to explain how human knowledge is created and transmitted. Trevarthen took the word and made it his own. In a paper he wrote in a book to honour the linguist Michael Halliday he said *'like Halliday and Habermas I believe that intersubjectivity or the mental representation of self-plus-other is the key to human kind of communication*' (in Steele & Threadgold 1987: 180).

For Trevarthen the complex intersubjectivity of infancy, before the development of speech, proves that linguistic forms of intersubjectivity are built on, and remain influenced by, preverbal forms of communication.

You will remember how Trevarthen began his research using the same technique as Daniel Stern, which was to analyse frame-by-frame the face-to-face interactions where both partners, adult and infant, are visible at the same time, free to act as they please for each other. In such an analysis numbers identify each frame of the film or television recording, and each frame lasts for a fraction of a second. This micro-descriptive technique, which Trevarthen first employed in his work with Martin Richards in Bruner's Research Programme at Harvard, allows the researcher to follow the interaction in minute detail through time, noting where one partner leads and the other follows. In his detailed analysis Colwyn looked for many features and events of everyday human expression, including lip and tongue movements, head turns, eye movement, hand gestures, finger movements and pointing. Later in this chapter you can read more about the special significance of pointing.

At the same time as Stern and Trevarthen were making their discoveries, Bateson (1979) micro-analysed film of mothers and infants recorded by Margaret Bullowa to study the development of language. It was Bateson who introduced the term *protoconversations* for the mini dialogues she observed and analysed and admired for their grace and 'ritual courtesy'. Stern *et al.* (1975) drew attention to the fact that the vocal exchanges were both coactive (which means taking place at the same time or concurrently) as well as alternating (taking place one after another). In other words mother and baby may vocalise not only in alternation, but also at the same time, in deliberate synchrony. This provides the foundation for two different functions of movement in communication – the first being a sympathetic joining of state or quality of emotion, sense of self and affectionate bonding, and the second being the deliberate sequential or the 'serial ordering' of purposeful projects such as those involved in logic.

The key mechanisms of interpersonal coordination

Interpersonal coordination (or the ways in which people match their movements, gestures, action, words and more to one another) may be a fundamental component of human social interaction. It is how they are able to make sense in cooperative, or not, ways.

Mother–infant communication is characterised by two forms of coordination; the first is called interactional synchrony and is focused on the shared pace and rhythm of communication, sometimes called 'mutual entrainment'. Some theorists speak of this being like a metaphorical dance between infant and caregiver. As Bateson showed, it looks, feels and acts like a conversation, although no words are uttered by the baby. It is a two-way interaction of movements that has two active and imaginative contributors. The interactions are rhythmic and mutual, with the baby and caregiver seeming to be in harmony as they take turns making similar sounds and show similar emotions and behaviours. It is evident that each partner in the dyad can anticipate how the other will behave and can elicit a particular response from them. You can recognise this synchrony immediately when the mother smiles at the baby who is making a smile-like movement, or opens her mouth in surprise when the baby pulls a scrunched up expression. Synchrony means a simultaneous movement or action: interactional synchrony relates to the timing and/or pattern of an exchange. The interaction or give-and-take is necessarily rhythmic and may or may not include the infant and caregiver mirroring each other's behaviour or emotion, sympathetically.

The second form of interpersonal coordination is known as behavioural matching/mimicry and focuses on the co-occurrence (which means taking place at the same time) or imitation of gross and fine motor movements sometimes called the chameleon effect. Condon and Sander (1974) looked at how babies' movements relate to the speech of the mothers. They found that as early as the first day of life the neonate moves in what they call '*precise and sustained segments of movement*' that are synchronised to the speech sounds of the adult. Take a moment to think about how remarkable this is. Condon has studied the broad categories that define the ways in which human individuals of any age engage in interpersonal coordination during social interactions. When I searched for an example of interpersonal synchrony, what came up was people dancing the tango. I liked that because it enabled me to see two people matching their moves and feelings to one another. When I searched for behavioural mimicry, what emerged was the automatic imitation of movements, posture, gesture, sounds and styles of speech.

Learning to point

We are taking a step away from Trevarthen to examine the work of Raymond Tallis, a fine writer and intellectual, researcher into neuroscience and a poet and philosopher.

His book called *Michelangelo's Finger* is on the significance of pointing – one of those gestures we all make as part of communicating with others. In the Foreword to the book he says this:

> *Over time, the repeated and multiple effects of a slight difference can make a big difference. The independent movement of the index finger is one such small and easily overlooked thing, and it has made a big difference. We sometimes need thinkers of genius to make us see this. Michelangelo was such a thinker, although he usually thought with a paintbrush and chisel rather than a pen. The Creation of*

Adam, one of his frescoes on the ceiling of the Sistine Chapel in Rome, is one of the most familiar images in Western art, depicting if you believe the story, the most important event in the history of the universe. Yes, God had been pretty busy up to that moment. In just five days he had instructed the void to shape up; had commanded light to come into being and stand in tidy rows of days and nights; had divided the water from the land and heaven from the earth; had summoned grass and beasts and the sun and the moon and the stars into being ... and created man in His own image. ... At the centre of the picture are two fingers separated by a small gap: the index finger of God's right hand; and the index finger of Adam's left hand.

(2011: xiii–xxiv)

Tallis is witty and clever and his book will make you smile, but some of what he says, drawn from his own experience, is thought provoking and relevant. He tells us how his first child, at the age of ten months, before having any significant language, started to point at things.

 Think about this

Why do children point?

In his book, Tallis (2011) explains his astonishment at what his child – and all other children – are doing when they point at things. Children may point at things that attract their attention – perhaps because they are pleasing or interesting, unfamiliar or frightening, surprising or exciting. They point at something in order to share their feelings with someone else. They point *at* in order to point *out*. Very soon after they start to point they begin to ask 'wazatt?'

The communication between the mother and infant often takes place around a topic or something that interests them both. Murray (2014) tells us that primary caregivers use particular facial and vocal cues that have an ostensive quality during these interactions. In linguistics the word ostensive means denoting a way of defining by direct demonstration: pointing is one way of doing this. We talked about ostensive marking in the previous chapter where nine-month-old Isabel was helped to understand her mother's goals and interests by her mother giving her various signals at key points of action – looking at things, smiling, vocalising and, of course, pointing.

Pointing is almost universal but there is a body of evidence that suggests that autistic children may not point in the same way that other young children do. Tallis (2011) tells us that Charlotte Moore, the mother of two autistic children, wrote that they did point but they mainly only did so when asked to. What is significant is that they very rarely pointed in order to share attention.

Summing up Section 2

We have come to the end of the first year of life. The infant is now able to share the intentions and feelings and experiences of others. She can make and share meanings with them, collaborate with them and work on joint projects. She uses movement and gesture, sounds and actions and expressions and is beginning to use words and this admits her to other worlds, new people and endless exploration and discovery. In the words of the musicologist Bjørkvold:

> this little social being dramatically enlarges his or her world during the first year of life. At every step of the way, bodily movement, rhythm, and the intonation of language are of decisive importance. ... During the second year of life the child's interest turns increasingly toward other children, especially those of similar age. ... Once the process begins, it moves quickly. First there is one playmate, then a large group; first one game, then many. A magical new chapter opens for the child during the third year of life, one of companionship, as well as loneliness, in the company of other children in play.
>
> (Bjørkvold 1991: 16–19)

Section 3

From one to three

Earlier in this book we looked in some detail at the experiences that infants have had with others they know and love in the first year, before they can understand and use spoken language. To do this we have looked at the significance of movement, gesture, expression and vocalisation during neonatal interactions with a primary caregiver; the vocalisations of both caregiver and infant in protoconversation; the making and sharing of meaning and the developing ability to cooperate on tasks and join in activities with interesting rules and tools. By the time the human infant reaches the second year of life she is also beginning to understand and use the words of the language or languages of her home. She begins to talk. By the time she turns four she may well have a broad vocabulary and be able to describe, question, explain, invent worlds, link episodes into narratives, answer, discuss, invent and use the rules of her language. In this section we will examine Trevarthen's views on how this expanding of the infant's social and practical world happens, and relate his ideas to those of his predecessors and contemporaries.

Chapter 3.1

Beginning to talk

The communicative child

By now you will almost certainly know that from very early on in life the human infant shows a unique communicative pattern of behaviour with a body adapted for sharing ideas. From the moment of birth she pays close attention to the sounds of her mother's or other primary caregiver's voice, facial expressions and hand movements. The newborn not only listens and pays attention to the rhythms and tones of words spoken to her but also responds to these. So communication begins.

Trevarthen draws on the work of Bateson (1975), who, you may remember, closely examined the development of communication from early infancy, perceiving these interactions as protoconversational. When looking at early interactions she noticed that when the infant responded or used pre-speech mouth movements accompanied by gesture – vocalising and gesturing at the same time – the response of the mother was not only positive, but almost always verbal. This response – with speech being something recognised or accepted as speech – indicated that the infant's response was taken as both verbal and meaningful by the mother. An examination of filmed dyadic interactions such as those that amazed Bateson revealed that the interactions were not always symmetrical, and the babies were certainly not just listening and watching. They were active participants in a social, cultural, human act of communication. It showed that very young babies could lead and even control the interaction. So the communicative efforts of the baby are not only precursors of language but can function in directing communication with adults. In other words the infant does not just listen to or receive speech but sometimes initiates it and leads the exchange.

By the end of the first year of life it is very apparent that the infant wants and needs to have things labelled or named for her. She points at objects, peers closely at them or holds them up with an implied question, 'What is this thing called?' She needs the label so that she can use it herself.

How children acquire language is a vexed question and has been researched by many people over many years. To appreciate where Trevarthen stands in the debate we need to look at the ideas of some of those whose work influenced him in one way or another.

Halliday and Chomsky

To assess Trevarthen's views on language acquisition, read the piece cited below:

> To understand how language can share intentions, experiences and feelings, and how it must be represented widely in the brain, we recognise that the sense of words is transmitted to a child initially by rhythmically patterned movement of the whole body, and is taken up by perceptive response to other person's self-related feelings for their experiences and prospects of action. Language is a function of intersubjective resonance of conscious embodied agency and aesthetic and moral emotions. All these requirements have manifestations in a newborn infant, and they can be traced back to species-specific organic and psychological capacities emerging in the human embryo and fetus. We are made for sympathetic cooperative creativity, and we learn words to define its purposes.
>
> (Delafield–Butt & Trevarthen 2013: 214).

On first reading it is quite difficult to understand exactly what the authors are saying. We can find evidence that they see the origins of language in the movements of the whole body; movements that are patterned and rhythmical. Language is clearly also rooted in emotion and feelings. And it is species specific – animals do not have language per se. It arises out of engagements with others of the same species, engaged in making and sharing meaning. But let's start by looking at two of the most influential thinkers on the subject of early language learning: Michael Halliday and Noam Chomsky.

Michael Halliday was a sociolinguist, interested in the usefulness of spoken language for the community. He talked of language development rather than language acquisition, which was the term used by Noam Chomsky. Halliday's view is closer to that of Trevarthen because he appreciated the significance of recognising that language – being an infinite, variable and dynamic resource for making and sharing meaning – is constructed and maintained through interaction with others. These interactions, he believed, took place primarily between the primary caregiver and infant in the first few months of life. He said that what takes place in these very early interactions is an exchange of attention. There may be no 'content' or subject to these exchanges but they are about feelings and have meaning. In other words they may not be about anything in particular, but they matter and they allow for the expression of feelings. He emphasised two points: language is a system for making meaning, and meaning is created in the process of mutual exchange. Halliday (1993) was the first to use the word protolanguage for these early shared attention episodes. He went on to say that these early exchanges, during the first six months of life, are inter-subjective, between thinking minds of acting people. When the child starts vocalising and gesturing, pointing and focusing on objects and people in the world, the exchanges are no longer simply about inner subjective feelings, but about and with the outside 'real' world and the people and objects in it. When children are engaged in interactions with others, two things may happen: the focus of attention can be explored *with* another in order to understand better, or explored *through* another in order to bring about some change. Halliday called these ways of engagement the *reflective* and the *active*. Reflective attention is shared vocally while active attention is shared gesturally. Trevarthen was clearly impressed by Halliday's work and refers to it frequently in his talks and writing.

When we move on from protolanguage to thinking about language itself, Halliday says we have to consider the development of a *semiotic* system. Semiotics is the study of signs and symbols – what they mean and how they are used. Language is made up of *semantics* (which is meaning), *syntactics* (the formal properties of signs and symbols in combination – the rules or grammar) and *pragmatics* (which is the study of language in social contexts). Halliday's work is very interesting but sometimes technical and difficult to read.

Noam Chomsky, a radical American thinker and writer, was the first to suggest that language acquisition is genetically or biologically determined. This view holds that the human infant is born with a special intelligence, pre-programmed to generate and work with the rules of spoken language. Every language has to be rule-bound in order for the users of the language to be able to both make and share meaning. The rules of English are not the same as those of Mandarin or Hindi, for example. If you are interested in this approach – and some of it is very persuasive and important – you can easily read more about his work.

We know that Bruner supported Trevarthen to begin his research on infant behaviour and intelligence and that they shared ideas and values. Bruner was influenced by aspects of Chomsky's work, but felt that he totally ignored the significance of the roles of others in the development of language. Essentially Bruner held that for language to develop, at least two people had to be involved in some sort of exchange and negotiation. Where Chomsky proposed the existence of an inbuilt *Language Acquisition Device (LAD)*, Bruner elaborated this to become a more sociocultural model – the *Language Acquisition Support System (LASS)*, which he saw as being like an adult scaffolding system. Children learn language through their interactions with more experienced others who cue the children's responses and share meanings with them in particular contexts and within a culture. Trevarthen, likewise, did not accept that the acquisition of language could be understood as separate from the understanding of persons and a consciousness of their whole presence and feelings. He said the only 'language acquisition device' is a baby engaged with companions (Trevarthen 1998a).

What, then, makes the ideas of Trevarthen about how children come to learn their language and culture innovative? Like all human beings asking questions about the world and the people in it, Trevarthen drew on his own experience as a child, an adolescent and an adult to find answers. His experience, you will remember, was that of being a young natural scientist learning about plant and animal life, a physiologist and then a neurophysiologist. This accounts for his broad knowledge of aspects of development that link us to our ancestors in the animal world – their imaginative powers of movement, for example. When he went to work with Bruner in a project studying how infants perceive and learn, this confirmed his interest in the process of development and gave him an opportunity to develop a working knowledge of how to make and analyse film clips of infant behaviour. And in all his years of academic research and writing he certainly read and often met key thinkers in the field. What makes his work unique, I would suggest, is the pulling together of these different strands to produce a different picture of how children come to know, or grow, their language and their culture.

Words and more words

Around the time of her first birthday the child begins to use the words she has learned whenever possible and begins to join words together to ask questions, make demands, express feelings and communicate in all possible situations. Some children speak fluently very early on and others take their time. There is a story, possibly apocryphal, that Albert Einstein did not say a word until the age of about five and when prompted to speak by his worried mother responded with asking 'Can I say anything, or must it be relevant?' A very subtle response showing excellent use of words.

Children start by using the sounds related to the words in their immediate world, which might be the names of people or objects or places. They hear, recognise and respond to words referring to people or objects or places. They begin to develop a vocabulary related to their culture, home, family and neighbourhood. Sofia, learning to speak both Italian and English, struggled for a time with making the sounds but mastered the gestures, the hand movements and the expressions of rural Italy – the non-verbal communication – like an expert. The Russian author Kornei Chukovsky became fascinated by how the young child acquires language, and he collected examples of the things children say at home, on the beach, in bed, during the day and as they fall asleep. His little book *From Two to Five* was published in 1963 and was out of print for many years but, if you can find a copy of it, it makes for very entertaining reading. His work led him to state that young children, under the age of five, before they go to school, use language creatively and he described them as being little linguistic geniuses. Here is what he said about language acquisition: *'The young child acquires his linguistic and thinking habits only through communication with other human beings'* (1963: 9).

Think about this

Read this short piece written by Vivian Gussin Paley, one of the truly great educators and observers of young children, who recorded events in her nursery class and wrote a series of wonderful books. She was determined that the young children in her kindergarten could and should create and live out their own stories. Read this tiny extract between Wally and Eddie and decide what it tells you about young children's thinking.

> *Wally:* When you're little you try to think of what the name of something is and people tell you.
> *Eddie:* Oh, yeah. Your mother tells you. You come out of her stomach and she talks English to you and she tells you the name for everything.
>
> (1981: 116)

Out of the mouths of babes! A small child who understands exactly how he and all the people he knows have come to speak the languages they do.

Revisiting communicative musicality

Earlier in this book we discussed the theory of communicative musicality and I want to return to this now because Trevarthen, together with collaborators including Gratier and Malloch, spent time and thought analysing early interactions using the musical terms of pitch, intonation and cadence. When children begin to learn and use individual words, which they then elaborate into sentences, their early experience of playing with pitch, intonation and cadence comes to the fore.

Think about this

My father – who was neither English nor Scottish – would chant these words to us when we were little, and far too young to understand the words, merely in order to make us excited, fearful, and thrilled to join in … 'It was a dark and stormy night and the captain said "Jock, pick up thy musket" and Jock began … "It was a dark and stormy night …"' ad infinitum. From the time we were tiny children we were invited to join in using our voices making any sounds or noises we chose. The original song describes the captain inviting his mate to pick up the story, not his musket! I vividly remember the sounds of my dad's voice changing with each rendition of the invitation to join in.

It is evident that the development of human communication and language is a complex learning process that evolves from the beginning of life through daily social interactions combined with expressive movements and almost invariably with the primary caregiver. Through these face-to-face interactions the infant uses and elaborates her vocalising in both response to and provocation of a response from the partner in the exchange, and in this way develops a repertoire of changes in pitch, intonation and cadence. Gratier and Devouche (2011) showed that the development of infant vocal production is related to the contingent stimulation from adult caregivers, who selectively reinforce specific vocal features. In short, this means that the baby who repeats the sounds she hears from the mother is encouraged to develop her awareness of the sounds of her native language or languages.

Attention to the intonation and melodic patterns in parent–infant interaction lead to the development of the interdisciplinary research between musical physics and language, and to the theory of communicative musicality. There is a large body of work related to this now, which you can read if you find it particularly fascinating, as I do. For example it is interesting to know that in-depth acoustical analyses of early vocal interactions have revealed that musical qualities of mother–infant pitch patterns lead to moments of shared vocal engagement by what is sometimes called 'tonal synchrony' (Van Puyvelde *et al*. 2010). What this means is that the vocalisations of mothers and infants are related to each other according to the acoustical laws of tonality involving particular integer pitch-ratios of the harmonic series. This is rather too technical for us but I am returning to this stage of vocal play and exchange to set the scene for what comes next.

Trevarthen accepts that the protoconversational narrative, i.e. a non-verbal exchange, between a parent and preverbal child can be compared to the literary form of story with a purposeful 'introduction', 'development', 'climax' and 'resolution' or 'conclusion' (Trevarthen 2008). He is not suggesting that such a narrative is made up of conventional grammatical parts, but rather that it makes human sense.

 Think about this

A small task for you

You might remember reading the piece below earlier in this book and it is repeated here in order for you to be able to underline or highlight whatever individual words or phrases in relation to language that seem most significant for you.

> *Human sense is the understanding of how to live in the human and physical worlds that children normally develop in the first few years of life. It is learned spontaneously in the course of the direct encounters with these worlds that arise daily and unavoidably everywhere, transcending cultural differences. ... The learning is continually informed and guided by emotion – that is, by feelings*

of significance, of value, of what matters. And it is highly stable and enduring, once established. It is the foundation on which all that follows must build.
(Donaldson, personal communication)

Here are my key words/phrases: *learned spontaneously; direct encounters with these (physical) words that arise daily and unavoidably everywhere, transcending cultural differences; learning is informed and guided by emotion … and is of significance, of value, what matters; stable and enduring; the foundation on which all that follows must build.*

Trevarthen tells us that in communicative musicality these episodes of early dyadic interactions show that the dynamic emotions of human movement, as in walking, posing and making gestures, are expressed vocally and perceived by the same principles of motivation in infant and parent. We know that mothers in all cultures speak in musical or dancing ways that interest and enchant infants, sometimes in order to amuse them, sometimes to calm them down, sometimes to invite them to smile and sometimes to close their eyes in sleep; sometimes to respond with rhythmic head movements, facial expressions, touching, stroking or bouncing. Niki Powers demonstrated these universal principles in her study of voice sounds of mothers playing with four-month-old babies in Scotland and Japan (Powers & Trevarthen 2009). By inducting the infant into the songs and games, stories and language, customs and values there is a sharing of feelings in story-telling ways that help build a loving bond that attracts the child into the community.

Vocal games and language: story and narrative

At about six months of age the sounds of speech in the 'mother tongue' will be copied as the baby starts to hear more subtle features and imitate them in vocal games (Powers & Trevarthen 2009). You will know of some of these; they occur in all languages and cultures. Some include small action songs like incy wincy spider climbing up the wall, or the teddy bear going round and round the garden. The baby listens and feels with attention to the pulse or the drama, waits with anticipation of the climax and joins in. Around the time of the first birthday, when the child has begun to attach names to people and objects she starts to make deliberate actions to attract the attention of others. She is on the verge of being a performer, seeking attention, approval and applause. In essence what she wants is response and confirmation of what she is knowing and doing. Gestural expressions may also become 'codified' in speech; for example, waving the hand may be replaced with the word 'bye bye'. The child beginning to use speech is involved in the language game – the intention to make acts of meaning, to interact with others and express feelings with others. Trevarthen (2011) quotes Daniel Stern (2000) in reminding us that this is '*a new development of intersubjectivity, or awareness of being a person with persons, and of a sense of self. It rests on trust and enjoyment of shared living in the family*'.

A toddler who is just beginning to speak in sentences has become expert at sharing experiences, commenting on events, taking poses, making jokes, imitating new ideas, sensing the style of performances. Trevarthen says that she can '*make up imaginary events and experiences, metaphorically, using body expressions of emotion in intentional sequences that are memorable*' (2011: 184). Turner (1996), in *The Literary Mind: The Origins of Thought and Language*, said that telling a story or making up a narrative may not be dependent on language, it is the other way round. An autobiographical story – your story – can only be told by you once you have shared your feelings with another and become a social self able to coordinate body movements in rhythmic time and have found an interested audience. If this interests you, you may want to read the wonderful book edited by Sylvie Rayna and Ferre Laevers called *Understanding the Under 3s and the Implications for Education*.

Bruner talks about the human need for stories and how teaching and learning depend on this:

> *Why are we so intellectually dismissive towards narrative?... Storytelling performs the dual cultural functions of making the strange familiar and ourselves private and distinctive. If pupils are encouraged to think about the different outcomes that could have resulted from a set of circumstances, they are demonstrating useability of knowledge about a subject. Rather than just retaining knowledge and facts they ... use their imaginations to think about other outcomes. ... This helps them to think about facing the future and it stimulates the teacher too.*
>
> (1996: 39–40)

 Think about this

Halliday recognised the expressiveness of non-verbal vocalisations and gestures and he charted the progress of his son through the first two years of life and was able to speak fluently. Halliday wrote down in phonetic script the sounds his son made in interaction with his mother, or while 'talking' to himself, and Halliday (1975) identified these developmental phases:

- Birth to 9 months, 'protoconversation', changing to 'conversation';
- 10 to 15 months, 'proto-language', changing to 'language';
- 15 to 20 months, 'proto-narrative and dialogue' changing to 'narrative;
- 20 months onwards, 'proto-discourse', describing imagined and remembered events.

Trevarthen argues, in agreement with Bruner, that human beings are story-seeking and story-making creatures from birth, and it is this that makes them find new and varied ways to express and share their feelings, thoughts and experience. Their sense of self develops through their interactions with others, sharing and making meaning. They are active participants in their communities and display interest and pleasure in looking at things, listening to sounds, imitating, cooperating and contributing to their culture. He argues that what practitioners working with young children seek to do primarily is to protect them when they might better be providing opportunities for them to play with one another, engage in story creation and adventurous play. As Paley says, *'for them* (the children) *friendship and fantasy already are broad avenues leading to questions and considerations that make sense to everyone'* (1988: viii–ix).

Gesture and language

Trevarthen continually reminds us that the movements we make with our hands and fingers, eyes and heads, combined with the facial expressions and vocalisations we use are all part of what enables us to become communicative partners with others. These are the ways in which we initiate, maintain and conclude interactions with others from the earliest days of life. To bring a smile to your face go to YouTube and look for 'Antonio baby talks with Nonna' to witness how dramatic, communicative and gesturally rich this little boy's protoconversation with his grandmother is. We all use gestures when we talk. We may not be aware of them or consciously making them but if you stop to look and listen you will start to see just how important our hands, in particular, are to conveying a message to someone else.

Susan Goldin-Meadow (2009) says that the gestures that accompany speech encode meaning differently from speech, in a complementary way. Gesture depends on showing something to another person. It is a visual means of communication. Speech, alone, consists only of words and grammatical devices. In establishing whether gesture can be considered as a language, Goldin-Meadow believes that only when gesture needs to carry the full burden of communication can it be considered a language. When it accompanies speech it shares the role of communication, especially the motives and energy of the story.

What we learn from gesture creation in deaf children

In her marvellous book, *The Resilience of Language*, Goldin-Meadow (2005) states that analysis of gesture creation in deaf children can tell us about how all children learn or create language. The book was first published in 2003 and is now in its second edition. It clarifies just what makes a system a language. Here are some of her findings:

- Before they produce the first recognisable signs, deaf children, exposed to sign language from birth, babble gesturally just as hearing children babble orally.
- Deaf children begin manual babbling at around the same age that hearing children begin their oral babbling.

- Manual babbling develops into the first signs just as oral babbling develops into the first words.
- Deaf children produce their first recognisable signs slightly earlier than hearing children produce their first true words. It is suggested that this may be because making a sign requires less fine motor control than making the first word.
- Early signs, like early words, are not usually referential. In other words they are not used to name or indicate objects and actions. It is only around the first birthday that both deaf and hearing children use signs and vocalisations to refer to objects and events.
- Children born in Manchester, for example, have the task of learning English whereas children growing up in Beijing face learning Mandarin. But deaf children face different tasks. Those living with parents using sign language are exposed to learning 'sign' as a different kind of medium for sharing meaning. Goldin-Meadow says that sign language is '*language by hand and eye rather than by mouth and ear*' (2005: 19).

But not all deaf children are born to deaf parents and this poses another set of issues for both parents and children. Many hearing parents of deaf children want them to be part of the 'normal' world of the hearing. In the United States there is strong evidence that many parents want their deaf children to be taught a visible English. It has taken many years for people worldwide to recognise sign languages as 'real' languages, motivated in the same way as spoken languages. The important point for us is that children denied any systematic input through speech or sign will create communicative systems that have real linguistic structure, function and content. They create their own sign language with which they can communicate their ideas and thoughts and feelings, ask questions, make demands, explain ideas and contribute. We are back to the notion of 'communicative competence'.

I do recommend *The Resilience of Language* as an easy to read book with its simple line drawings of children making signs, and a text that is very approachable.

From talk to narrative and beyond

We know that a toddler picks up language by doing things with others and noticing what others do with language. In this way the child is picking up language socially. And as we have learned from Goldin-Meadow this applies to hearing and deaf children. Trevarthen reminds us that once the child begins to use words the further development of her language depends not only on referential intentions and attentions (by pointing, questioning, showing and giving, for example) but essentially also relates to what she is feeling, experiencing and meaning. The young speaker imitates what she sees and hears, creates words for herself and begins to play with words – both their sounds and meanings.

My daughter Sam sat down opposite me and announced 'I am oppositing you' – an inventive but totally logical creation of a new word. The most fortunate toddlers will have had experience of songs and stories told and read, word games played, books to hold and explore. They begin to invent worlds for themselves and make-believe begins to play a role in their lives, in play and often shared. But even children less fortunate display a similar ability to create and inhabit imaginary worlds. By the time the toddler is ready to be in settings for very young children she reveals her linguistic genius.

 Think about this

Chukovsky (1963) offers us these examples of just this genius. Remember that he was collecting samples of the spoken language of Russian children. Read the two small examples of this below and try to see what they reveal about how and why the children are using words.

> A two-year-old child, taking a bath was making her doll dive into and out of the bath, saying 'There, she drowns-in ... now, she drowns-out' (1963: 7).

> A three-year-old boy asked 'Daddy, when I talked with you over the telephone, how did you manage to get into the receiver?' (1963: 30).

The first child is making the words she knows work for what she wants to share. The second child is using words in order to understand something he does not understand.

Thinking about intent participation learning

I want to start this chapter by asking you a question. The children we are looking at are still very young children – toddlers – and in our societies very young children are cared for in their homes and many also in special places of learning: nursery classes, nursery schools, creches, playgroups, pre-schools and more. My question is whether you think these are places where children need to be 'taught' things or should they be places where they continue to learn things in their own way?

It is a fine distinction but a very important one. In many western societies there is a strong tendency to measure learning, and this approach operates on the philosophy of thinking that we can be told or taught things: in other words we take in experience, information or knowledge and then become able to speak or write about it. The assumption is that we need instruction in order to learn. This is a cognitive-behaviourist approach, which is incompatible with what Trevarthen understands. By now you will know that he sees human beings as essentially active and feeling people, born with agency or initiative, and the urge and determination to make sense of our world. He says that *'Children and adults, both, are creatures evolved for artfully making sense of life together. That is the defining characteristic of human nature'* (Trevarthen 2013a: 4).

It is worth reading that through and deciding what your key word might be. For me, the key word in that statement is 'together'.

A little about the prehistory of early childhood

Trevarthen does not only draw on information from biology, physiology and neurophysiology but also on literature, philosophy, history and anthropology. In thinking about early childhood he returns not to his own childhood but to the lives of ancient hunter-gatherers in order to guess or intuit what early childhood might have been like. He states that hunter-gatherers had very light and agile bodies with skilful hands and brains very like our own. They probably lived in bands of up to about a hundred individuals; knew one another well and depended on cooperatively working the land in order to survive. Before creating spoken language they must have communicated their needs and feelings by gesture and sounds, in sharing the world and making objects and creating songs and dances to express themselves.

Their infants were born like ours and took many years to reach maturity. They were dependent on their mothers' milk for nutrition and their support and protection for survival for the two or three years after birth. There are artefacts remaining from their culture that reveal tools and ornaments, creations not only useful but also aesthetically pleasing. On these there are often symbols to record their ideas, affirm their beliefs and celebrate their communal rituals. Trevarthen speaks of these relics as relating to what he calls a '*special human form of playfulness*' (Trevarthen 2013a: 5).

Talking of playfulness and play

Nobody who is interested in babies and toddlers can fail to have thought about the meaning of the words playful and play. Play is about so much more than 'having fun' or 'messing about'. Those who make comments about a child 'just playing' clearly do not understand what play is and why it matters.

Trevarthen introduced me to the writings of Peter Gray – an anthropologist who has written a very significant chapter on what he calls a play-filled childhood in still existing hunter-gatherer communities. You can find it online or in *Evolution, Early Experience and Human Development: From Research to Practice and Policy* (Narváez 2012). Gray (2012) studied existing communities of what he calls <u>bands</u> of roughly 30–50 individuals. They are nomads, moving from place to place to follow game and vegetation. They all have very <u>egalitarian</u> social structures, decide things together, own little property, share food and material goods within and with other bands. Within these small communities Gray believes that their egalitarian ethos is maintained by cultivating the playful part of their human nature. Social play – where two or more people are engaged – is, by definition, egalitarian. You cannot play unless you suspend aggression and domination. You have to cooperate and share, collaborate and respect.

 Think about this

Here are the five features of play defined by Gray (2012).

- Play is self-chosen and self-directed. If someone tells you what to play or how to play you are not playing, but following directions.
- Play is intrinsically motivated – the player does it for herself. Vygotsky (1978) said it was '*an activity in which means are more valued than ends*'.
- Play is guided by mental rules. All play has rules and children, freely choosing to play, are in a situation where they must adhere to the rules of the games they are playing.

- Play is imaginative or, as Huizinga (1955) put it, play always involves some degree of psychologically removing oneself from the real world. The key words with regard to play are imagination, fantasy, pretend.
- Play involves an active, alert but unstressed frame of mind.

Keeping all of this in mind let us return to Trevarthen's phrase of intent participation learning and find some examples of it to make the meaning clear.

Barbara Rogoff has talked and written about what she calls *intent community participation*. What she means is how, in some communities, when children – even very young children – are included in community activities where they can observe, contribute and get support and feedback from others, they are accepted as members of the community and learn alongside more expert others about the world using the tools of their culture. They are not being taught but invited to participate in a meaningful and engaging task. Her ideas developed after working in a Mayan community in Guatemala. There she noticed that the young children seemed to be very skilled and she asked the mothers how they had taught the children. The mothers replied, 'We don't teach them, they learn.' Remember these words. The children, engaged in the real-world activities of their families and culture, can join in as full partners and, because the activities are significant to their lives, will do so with intent.

I looked up synonyms for intent and here are some of the ones I found: *engrossed, absorbed, attentive, captive, hell-bent, eager* and *concentrated on*. This gives a flavour of how the children respond when they are involved in something that interests them and has meaning and purpose for them.

Trevarthen, having spent years observing newborn babies and toddlers in the real settings of everyday life, borrowed aspects of this term to create his version: intent participation learning. This is very close to Rogoff's term in the sense of children being very engaged and involved in something with others. The word 'community' is inferred, and is supplemented by 'learning'. The implication is that young children are most likely to be engaged and involved in learning about experience when they are playing, which often, but not always, involves at least one other person.

Defining the three contributory words of the phrase 'intent participation learning' might make its meaning clearer. 'Intent' means with interest or determination or eager attention. 'Participation' means joining with at least one other. And 'learning' means – well, it depends on where you stand on the continuum related to the habits of schooling – from being taught facts and skills in a formal way, to Donaldson's view that learning is always guided by emotion, which means by feelings of significance, of value, of what matters

 Think about this

Vivian Gussin Paley, whom I have already mentioned as one of the giants of early childhood, was a teacher who found she had to learn about learning.

She became a kindergarten teacher in the United States and at first did what she was asked to do until the day a high school science teacher asked if he could spend time with the young children in the kindergarten. He had a grandchild about to enter nursery school and he wanted to know how to teach such young children. He very quickly established an amazing rapport with the children and Paley noticed that he talked to the children and listened to the children and, most importantly, he was truly curious to hear their ideas and thought. Paley realised that what he was doing was being genuinely interested in what the children were saying, and that was the starting point for all that followed. From that day Paley turned her classroom into a place where the children determined what to do. She offered them opportunities for endless play. They learned as they played with intent participation.

Intent musical participation

It will not surprise you that this – the ability to engage intently, if briefly – is apparent immediately after birth when the infant engages in tiny episodes of communication. You will remember that Trevarthen and his colleagues (Malloch and Gratier, in particular) talked of communicative musicality where the newborn baby and mother were able to synchronise rhythms, use expressive gestures and qualities of voice like pitch and cadence. Much later, within a few of months of the end of the first year of life and before speech, the baby becomes more able to engage in cooperative person–person–object awareness or, to use the language of Trevarthen, secondary intersubjectivity.

A fortunate infant will have engaged in joining in and listening and responding to some of the many thousands of children's songs and rhythmic games evident in all cultures and languages. She may have witnessed musical games and jokes that invite her to join in with movement and voice. She may have developed the confidence to perform the actions she has recently mastered: perhaps clapping her hands, waving her arms, dancing or vocalising for herself or to an audience. She becomes a true participant in her musical community. In the second and third years of life the role of music in the child's community will, to some extent, determine her engagement with it. I was interested to note that music features significantly in the post-apartheid programme for pre-school children in South Africa. In China young children are taught music in a very formal way from very early childhood.

Older toddlers watch and listen with great concentration and then take pleasure in copying and participating in musical activities. They begin to make music in one way or another with their peers, copying rhythms and actions, sounds and pitch. The development of spoken language at this time is often accompanied by the child hearing nursery rhymes and simple poems.

Trevarthen and Malloch (2002) tell us that research on baby songs in different languages confirms that these songs give guidance towards speech sounds in the mother tongue, particularly the vowels, which are affect-laden tones. Affect-laden means weighed down by emotion. Small children enjoy playing with the sounds of singing and there are patterns in baby songs that help children attend to the placing of vowel sounds and rhymes. Daniel Stern (2010) said that the mother's animated speech to her child acted as a 'dynamic proto-narrative envelope'. This term is much used in psychoanalysis and may be difficult to grasp. In essence it refers to the scaffolding or story-shaping role the mother performs with an emotional voice that helps her infant acquire language. Malloch and Trevarthen (2000, 2009) refer to the nursery rhymes and songs as 'emotional narratives'.

Intent expressive participation

When very young children get deeply involved in what they are doing some theorists talk about the skills they are acquiring and the cultural and physical tools they are becoming familiar with. This is happening, of course, but it is really a small part of the story. Early mark-making is essentially about communicating and representing feelings and thoughts through actions and vocalisations. John Matthews (1994), in his seminal and very personal book, tracked how his own children, Ben, Joel and Hannah, expressed themselves through painting and drawing. Matthews is, himself, an artist and a teacher and he quotes Trevarthen throughout the book. In considering visual representation and expression, Matthews reminds us that newborn babies are able to share in acts of meaning with primary caregivers. They also appear to come into the world with a simple understanding about events and objects and their mastery of objects occurs through their interactions with significant others around the objects.

 Think about this

Ben, aged two, stands at a low table on which there is a sheet of paper and two pots of paint, one green and one blue. In each pot stands a paint brush. First of all, Ben picks up the blue brush with his right hand and paints with it, using a vigorous fanning action from side to side across the surface of the paper. ... Ben then puts this blue brush back in the pot and picks up the green brush. As he carries it over the painting, paint drips from it, leaving a trail of green spots across both the table and the painting. He notices this and immediately shakes the brush above the painting, making more green spots fall into the white paper. In the meantime Linda, his mother, has prepared a pot of red paint for him and has placed it with a brush inside on the table next to the other two pots. Picking up the red brush he makes further arcing movements over the blue patch. The red mixes with the blue to make a brownish colour. He momentarily stops painting, and points with his left index finger to a particular part of the painting. The focus of attention appears to be a section of the painted patch's irregular edge which his paintbrush has just produced. 'There's a car there,' he says.

(Matthews 1994: 13)

Matthews asks the question of how we can understand what it is that little Ben is doing when he paints. Could he be 'babbling'; in paint just as babies babble pre-speech? He clearly know something about paints and how they work and from his first attempts his complete engagement with what he is doing is evidence that what he is doing is communicating his feelings. But when he 'finds' a car in his painting is he also exploring the possibilities of representation?

Making marks is something that all children in all cultures do and they use whatever is at hand to make marks. You will have seen babies using a finger in wet sand or on a misted window, or a stick in damp earth; a pencil on paper, paints on the wall.

Intent physical participation

The toddler, with increasing mobility, begins to be able to participate physically as her range of actions expands. She can climb and jump and swing and dance, and loves to do all these things. She might be able to drive a toy car, throw and catch a ball, climb to the top of the slide and come down on it. She can show off these new skills and enjoy the praise she receives for her adventurous experimentation. She can use her hands with more confidence and skill, now able to draw and paint and cut and write and build. With these hands she gains experience of how different surfaces may feel and begins to understand the world of texture. She broadens the range of her vocal skills and shows them off in her performances of songs known and invented. At the same time she is increasing her vocabulary of spoken words extremely rapidly and begins a lifetime of making and telling stories. She might spend time looking at books, turning the pages and re-telling the stories she has had read to her. All of this takes place in the social world where she has other children and adults to use as models to be imitated, for confirmation of her own performances, to provide her with support she needs or comfort if things go wrong. She is on the verge of being able to create and inhabit invented worlds and to come to the point of symbolic behaviour.

Intent symbolic participation

As the child, in her second year of life, begins to speak she also develops her social awareness. She takes notice of others around her and of what they are doing and with what. Although she has already encountered play with objects in interactions with caregivers and others, as her social world expands she takes note of what older children and adults are doing and is very happy imitating them. The French psychologist Jacqueline Nadel has explored the role of imitation in the toddler's world and shown how a group of children too young to use talking can make and share fanciful meanings by moving together as a group of actors, inspiring one another by inventing endless games of imitation.

In the famed nursery schools in Reggio Emilia every *asilo nido* (nursery school) has a studio with a working artist in it. The children are free to wander in and out of the studio to watch or join in. They are able to use the cultural tools available to them to express their feelings or ideas, their pleasure and their fears. These nurseries are set in a culture that values the arts and seeks to enable children to be artful. In other places the emphasis might be on music or on the world of fantasy. Watching children draw and paint, dance and sing, play musical instruments, create and become actors in made up worlds, you see how intent and absorbed they can be as they make something that is important and meaningful to them and their friends, and also leave a record of what they have done and felt.

Young children, with their eagerness to imitate, reveal their desire to know more and gain skills from those more experienced than they are. As their experience of spoken language increases they want to talk and hear others talk about what they have done or made. Comenius, the seventeenth-century educator, said:

> *My aim is to show, although this is not generally attended to, that the roots of all sciences and arts in every instance arise as early as in the tender age, and that on these foundations it is neither impossible nor difficult for the whole superstructure to be laid; provided always that we act reasonably as with a reasonable creature.*
>
> (cited in Trevarthen 2004: 37)

At about one year of age the infant, together with peers, begins to negotiate what social roles to adopt in their games. They mimic and imitate observed symbolic behaviour. They might pretend to pour the tea or cut the bread or wield a knife or drive a car. This is symbolic play where one thing is made to stand for another. Turn-taking comes before such symbolic play. The ability to make one thing stand for or represent another is very significant in the sense that many of our systems for communication are made up of symbols. Think about written language – it is made up of words, which are made up of letters.

A very young child, as young as one year old, is able to work out that it might be possible and useful to imitate the ways in which another person speaks and acts. There is a lovely video clip of Helen becoming the manager of a cafe and changing her stance, her voice and the very ways of speaking that she has guessed is how a manager would sound. Symbolic behaviour is about more than changing just superficial aspects of behaviour. It is a much more complex set of behaviours of observing, internalising and then practising social acts in order to play out a role. Trevarthen says that '*all of human culture, including language, depends on creative imagination for moving with intelligence and a preference for sharing ideas and projects*' (Trevarthen 2013: 281). In this way the child is able to try out what it feels like to be strong, frightened, brave, angry, loving and more. And this is the foundation not only for forms of art and habits or ritual performances, but also for the grammar and rules of language – doing things with words.

The role of adults in intent participation

Barbara Rogoff is interesting on this subject. Having worked throughout much of the Americas and beyond her attention has been drawn to how children learn through interactions with others, always set in the context of everyday lives in their own communities and cultures.

 Think about this

Read through what she says here and think about what implications there are for those working with very young children.

> Children everywhere learn by observing and listening-in on activities of adults and other children. Learning through keen observation and listening, in anticipation of participation, seems to be especially valued and emphasised in communities where children have access to learning from informal community involvement. They observe and listen with intent concentration and initiative, and their collaborative participation is expected when they are ready to help in shared endeavours.
>
> (Rogoff et al. 2003: 176)

Think about how the children you know learn in their homes and in the homes of family members and friends. They learn primarily from looking and listening in real-life situations set in the safe and supportive environment of their home community. Supported in all their efforts they select what to focus on and join in with all the means at their disposal. Trevarthen said that

> Infants under one year, who have no language, communicate much more powerfully and constructively with receptive adults than psychological science of rational processes has expected ... they rapidly develop skilful capacities for regulating intimate encounters with humour, teasing and moral evaluations of different persons.
>
> (2011: 176)

Loris Malaguzzi, the founder of the preschool provision in Reggio Emilia, had an absolute belief in the curiosity and competence of babies, born into a world with other people in it where, as Trevarthen said, '*the art of sympathetic and creative two-way communication is essential for intent participative learning at every stage of teaching, from kindergarten to university*' (2011: 175–176).

The role of the adults living or working with very young children is interesting and sometimes challenging. There is in many adults, who have been 'well trained', the urge to adopt a didactic role – to teach, or tell, or show the child things so the child will learn. It might very well work, but only if what is being taught is of interest and importance to the child. Matthews is very astute about how important it is for the adults involved in their children's activities and attempts to be genuinely interested in what it is they are doing, why they are doing it, who it is being done for. It follows that the adults should ensure that their interest in the matter and manner of teaching and learning is genuine. They need to really pay attention so that they know what it is the child is doing and they need to follow the child's lead. For the child to be deeply engaged, the child has to be in control of the task and the outcome. There can be no right or wrong, good or bad. It is all about exploration, trying things out and seeing what happens.

Do you remember Stern's 'narrative envelopes'? In his analysis of one of his daughter's painting sessions with her mother, Matthews records that mother and child are in what he calls deep states of empathy with one another (1994: 130) in the envelope of space between them. Trevarthen reminds us that there is a biologically standardised time base for patterns of action like those of Matthew's little girl Hannah painting with her mother Linda. They move together and when one changes the speed or pace of the other is likely to follow – to keep in step.

Chapter 3.3

Companionship and loneliness

In this chapter we examine the growing child's need for companionship or friendship, and we also look at the evidence that even very young children experience the sadness of loneliness. It follows that one of the key themes to explore is the role of emotions in the life of the developing child. We have considered aspects of this with regard to young babies earlier in this book. We now look at the need at all ages for the support of the self in companionship that underpins Trevarthen's thinking about how we learn meaning.

In order to contextualise this, and situate it in a paradigm that might relate to Trevarthen's psychobiological perspective, we start by looking at some of the things we know from neuropsychology by going back to investigate what is happening in the brain when it is developing so the child can act with awareness and feelings, and learn.

Back to the brain and body

At this point it seems important to return to what is known about what may be observed to happen in the growing brain as the young child develops. In order to do that I will briefly explore the psychobiology of the child's attachment and emotional needs. I have drawn quite heavily on what you can find at http://developingchild.harvard.edu/wp-content/uploads/2015/05/Science_Early_Childhood_Development.pdf (National Scientific Council on the Developing Child, 2007).

Modern brain science knows that the architecture of the brain is constructed through an ongoing process that begins before birth and continues through adulthood. During the early years of life it appears that an astounding 700 new synapses or neural connections are formed every second. This is followed by a period when these connections between nerve cells are reduced through 'pruning'. This cutting back of connections appears to enhance the efficiency of the brain. What is important for us when we are thinking about education is to know that the child's early experiences affect the nature and quality of the brain's changing architecture and use of experience by determining which circuits are reinforced and which are pruned. A circuit is reinforced when the child experiences a positive feeling when the behaviour activated is 'successful', and pruned or lost when there is no response or a negative feeling. The researchers at Harvard refer to this as 'use it or lose it', but it is important to focus on the feelings that go with success or failure of what the mind wanted to do with movements of the body. Using is rewarding, and losing hurts.

The way in which brains are built can be regarded as hierarchical, starting with the basic core circuits and then moving up to more intricate circuits that react to and store experience. So sensory pathways like those that appreciate basic seeing and hearing and how they change when the body is active are the first to develop in early childhood, followed by mastery of cultural habits and everyday language skills, and then, at least for some of us, what are considered more 'clever' cognitive functions or creative reasoning and 'scientific' curiosity and higher cognitive function. Connections are formed and pruned throughout the growing brain in a prescribed, natural order: the timing of stages of learning is determined by the developmental process itself but this process changes when the child's experiences affect this or the feelings of success or failure determine whether the circuits of new habits are strong or weak. The brain is never a blank slate waiting to be written on by some author. Every new competency is built upon the competencies that came alive before in the busy brain with its sense of needs and of risks in body movement. Relationships are always important.

Scientists now accept that a major feature of the developmental process is what is known in the United States as the 'serve and return' relationship between children and their parents or other caregivers in the family or community. We know a great deal about this development in attachments from the work of Trevarthen on how, from the moment of birth, the infant is intent on communicating motives and feelings with the primary caregiver. The infant seeks and almost invariably gets a response as the chain of interaction continues.

Charles Nelson (2000) divides the development of the human social brain into three periods as follows:

- *infancy*, where the mother is the socialising agent or assistant who guides the baby in becoming a member of her family and culture. Trevarthen insists that in this experience the baby is never passive and is sometimes the initiator of a new move in the exchange, and also that even a newborn in the first moments can engage with and benefit from the sympathetic company of someone who is not the mother.
- *juvenile*, where experience through play with peers (whilst the mother/ caregiver acts as a safe base) promotes development of empathy, which is understanding the feelings of others – Trevarthen would call this the 'sympathy' of an imitative peer companionship.
- *adolescence*, when the young person is occupied with the transition from the home to peer groups who are becoming skilled in knowledge and practices of a particular culture and concerned with reproduction and maintaining social status in the group.

Allan Shore (1997) has written widely on the subject of emotions in brain development and he cites evidence that both the self-sustaining vital functions (like eating and drinking, for example) and the affectionate love-regulated interpersonal neurobiology (in interactions with special others) are mediated more in the right hemisphere of the human brains of infant and mother, or in the right brains of infant and father. This side of the human brain is the most active and rapidly developing in infancy as it prepares the growing body and its functions and activities for survival, and for a life of learning in human company.

I like that phrase – learning in human company. You may remember reading about John Bowlby's work relating to attachment but have not, perhaps, come across what he calls the environment of evolutionary adaptedness (EEA). This describes the social-emotional, relational environment provided by primary caregivers, which shapes, for better or worse, the experience-dependent maturation of the brain systems involved in attachment. This takes place at a non-verbal affective level, and one can see that this puts great responsibility on a mother's affectionate care.

Stephen Porges (2011) developed what he called the 'polyvagal theory', which specifies two functionally distinct branches of the vagus, or tenth cranial nerve, to explain the social behaviours of mammals, how they signal their inner states of well-being or distress. All of the movements observed during protoconversations between mother and infant described by Bateson in 1979 – the movements of the eyes, facial expressions, changes of pitch in the voice, all movement of the muscles of the face, throat, jaws, lips, tongue – are controlled by motor neurons of the vagus and other cranial nerves that were evolved primarily for self-regulation and survival. They were developed for eating, for breathing, for circulating the blood by the beating of the heart and for directing awareness of the environment by the distance senses of seeing and hearing. They are all elaborated in human beings precisely to allow them to engage with others to share meaning, ideas and feelings. Trevarthen adds to this list of expressive organs the hands, which have evolved from the paws of forelimbs used for locomotion, and become 'manipulative', and then very significant in the transmission and exchange of ideas and feelings as well as for developing tools. He observes (as cited earlier) that hands and gestures so active in infancy can be regarded as having full language capacity.

You might like to consider the functions of dopamine, which is a compound produced in the body that serves in the brain of mammals as a neurotransmitter that enhances the mother's feelings when she gives birth. When a woman has a normal, healthy birth she wants to engage in intense bodily contact with the baby, holding, caressing and breast-feeding her, and intently communicating with her through gaze, touch and vocalising. There are, of course, mothers who are not able to have this intimate pleasure with their baby, as when in periods of postnatal depression, which, if extreme or extended can have serious consequences for the future relationship between child and mother, and for the child's learning and development. Trevarthen draws attention to the effects of pressures placed on modern mothers living with the excessive demands of earning a living, running a home and raising children. He says: '*The development of larger brains in humans may get in the way of warm mothering*' (2013: 210).

The brain and companionship

Trevarthen (2005) explains what has been learned through the development of functional brain imaging which, by making moving pictures of the spread of electrical activity through brain tissues, gives evidence of how much of the brain is busy when we are expressing ourselves to or with other persons and being aware of their human bodies and their expressions of intentions and feelings, movement, gesture, language, vocalisation and more. In a simple protoconversation, for example, there are large areas of the frontal and parieto-temporal cortex involved in both infant and parent. Emotions expressed on the face and in the voice are controlled primarily in the paralimbic neocortex of the right hemisphere. And, when we consider intersubjective awareness and communication, we find that all of the neocortical regions are involved. Trevarthen and Kenneth Aitken's *Intrinsic Motive Formation* (IMF) is a mapping of cortical functions in a neural system that has evolved to regulate the ways in which a human being is alert to the presence and thoughts, feelings and intentions of others. They describe the proper function of the IMF as being essential for our thinking and for our learning in communication.

> *Infants' expressions stimulate the development of imitative and reciprocal relations with corresponding dynamic brain states of caregivers. … Primordial motive systems appear in sub-cortical and limbic systems of the embryo before the cerebral cortex. … We propose that an 'intrinsic motive formation' (IMF) is assembled prenatally and is ready at birth to share emotion with caregivers for regulation of the child's cortical development, upon which cultural cognition and learning depend.*
> (Trevarthen & Aitken 1994: 599)

 Think about this

The IMF functions in various ways as follows:

- as initiator of action, so that the body moves first and the senses follow, confirming the intention;
- as regulator of the well-being of the body, its health and happiness;
- as communicator of motives by the movement of attentive organs of emotional expression;
- as regulator of cognitive growth by influencing the morphogenesis of neocortical circuits. Morphogenesis means the biological process that causes an organic life system to develop its shape and function.

Laid down initially in the human foetus during the first trimester of gestation, the IMF is an essential component of the sensory-motor systems that become involved in human communication through gesture and speech, song and dance or by writing, playing musical instruments or using manual or digital means to communicate thought and feelings. It is what guides the development and learning of the child's brain as the acceptor of ideas and thoughts and becoming part of a meaningful culture. Trevarthen (2005) arrives at some conclusions that some might find shocking. These are:

- It is our brains that tell our minds to prepare to move our bodies in sympathetic ways when we see, hear or feel the bodies of others move.
- Emotions or feelings are active states of agency in the minds of others transmitted by their expressions. They are reflected in activity of the perceiver's brain. For example, the mother frowns, the child is concerned or worried.
- Purposeful activities are what Trevarthen calls 'adventures' with emotional and emotive drama imagining the future, not just ways to solve problems or simplify situations.
- The brain 'feels' emotions in preparation for moving, thus anticipating the feelings of effects of movement, not pushed by sensory evidence of the body.

Some theorists believe that the malfunctioning of the IMF might be involved in autism, a subject on which Trevarthen has taken a firm position since 1993 when, with Ken Aitken, Despina Papoudi and Jacqueline Robarts, he wrote *Children with Autism: Diagnosis, Prevalence in Scotland and Interventions that Meet Their Needs*, a Report to the Scottish Office, Department of Education.

 Think about this

Search for companionship

We have established that we humans are social animals and our young need to come to understand what those older than them in society are thinking, and in doing this must become able to discover and interpret signs of approval or disapproval. In simpler terms the young child has to understand the minds of others. Trevarthen says that this is why young children *'crave the consistent sensitive company of an affectionate parent or other person who can be trusted to sustain the shared memories that have been discovered in their company'* (2005: 64).

You might learn something important by underlining which are the key words for you in that statement.

Note: My underlined words in Trevarthen's statement above are 'consistent', 'sensitive company', 'affectionate', 'trusted', 'sustain', 'shared memories', 'discovered in their company'.

Through their encounters and interactions – or intersubjectivity – with others, young children come to understand aspects of the physical, emotional, social and symbolic worlds, and they do this sometimes through joint attention, sometimes through imitation, sometimes through play. The young child, after initially seeking intimate support for her physical comfort and well-being, moves on to seeking support in extending her skills and knowledge of the world, and her thinking, and does this in the company of more competent companions who are eager to interact with and support her pleasure in discoveries. Where these companions engage with interest and offer useful and positive feedback to the young child, the exchanges provide a source of affection, interest and joy. In talking of companions we are thinking of siblings, parents, grandparents, other children – any significant affectionate others in the child's life. It is obvious that while the child can engage regularly with another person to build a strong relationship, she may also enjoy shared expectations, a strong attachment and the ability to build a repertoire of shared actions and interests. Theorists who have closely observed young children insist that for this to happen there must be mutual <u>attunement</u>, shared affect and shared focus of interest. Judy Dunn (1988) wrote a perceptive analysis of the how young children develop an understanding of others. Her book *The Beginnings of Social Understanding*, although now quite dated, is easy to read and, in parts, gently amusing and very informative.

 Think about this

Dunn and Carol Kendrick (1982) carried out a study into communication among siblings and were enthralled with the story of 15-month-old Len and his younger brother. Len was a stocky boy with a large tummy and he loved pulling up his shirt in order to show off his tummy to his doting parents. It never failed to make them laugh. One day Len's older brother fell off the climbing frame and cried bitterly. Len watched and then approached his brother, pulling up his shirt and vocalising volubly (in Dunn 1988: 87–88).

 This is an example of a very young child being able to share and communicate with the experience and feelings of someone else. Not only that, but little Len has also made the link with his brother's pain and what he can draw on within himself to minimise that pain.

There are many examples of what is called 'deferred imitation' – which means that the child is repeating something she has observed and copied earlier, in order both to practise it, or sometimes simply to make contact and test the pleasure of relationships established with different people (e.g. Murray & Trevarthen 1986; Trevarthen 1990). There is, of course, the other side of the coin where the young child's attempts to interact are rebuffed or misunderstood perhaps by another child, or by a new adult who is ignorant of what the child knows and likes to do. The young child encountering or anticipating such a response may find it distressing and confusing. You will find out more about this when we consider feelings of shame.

In 2001 the Scottish Executive Education Department commissioned Trevarthen at the University of Edinburgh, and Helen Marwick at the University of Strathclyde, to write a report on how to meet the needs of children from birth to three in out of home provision – nurseries, playgroups, crèches and so on.

Looking at children in their second year of life, they noted that these children were beginning to develop an awareness of the meanings of others and could react emotionally to these. As an example they cite a child becoming fearful if misunderstood or confused when encountering conflicting meanings in what people say or do. The advice they offer to out of home facilities in terms of what they need to offer the children in terms of mixed-age or same-age opportunities for play is this: '*During this year children become more able to play imaginatively with company of different ages and can benefit from play with older children as well as peers*' (Stephen *et al.* 2003: 2).

The three Cs – companionship, culture and collaboration

Trevarthen allowed me to access the slides of some of his conference presentations and I have decided to summarise the talk he gave in November 2010 at a day conference entitled *Theology and Therapy* because it addresses the three Cs mentioned above.

In the past many rational thinkers and psychologists believed that we, as a species, can only be understood as being rational individuals. The new and more positive psychology of infancy held by Trevarthen and others says that our minds are born for sharing intentions, feelings and interests by moving in sympathy with others. As we have seen, our brains are motivated to express *mind states* as body movements and to communicate in the rhythm of common sense, called intersubjectivity. '*At birth the infant has special expressive and receptive organs adapted to monitor mental processes in the self and in others by keeping track of the prospective awareness made manifest in the shape and timing of movements*' (Trevarthen 2001, cited in Sightlines Initiative n.d.). Thus we communicate both motives and feelings, particularly sympathetic feelings, from birth, making sense of shared experience with attentive, communicative others. We know that this sharing is the foundation for building successful and positive relationships with others and for all learning. We also know the language is a learned code that gives us the most reliable bridge to the minds of others. More than that, it is the way in which we are able to analyse our own thoughts, ideas and feelings. In order to understand the feelings of others, however, we have to compare how they talk and behave with how we feel, behave and talk in shared exchanges.

You will remember that around nine months of age the baby becomes curious about what people are doing and what they are using to do it. This curiosity leads to them becoming able to follow directives, trying to make what Trevarthen calls *conventional messages* and trying to use objects as tools. This is all preparation for using language to label not only objects but also events, intentions and meanings. The children have been communicating from birth through sharing vocalising, gesture, hand signals, gaze, movement and more to reveal and share their feelings. Before they begin to talk they follow meanings with moral emotions such as pride in success, shame if not understood, joy in companionship, loneliness if rebuffed or misunderstood. By her first birthday the child can cooperate with common sense and use tools and enjoy the companionship of others. Having earlier developed the capacity to operate in three worlds, that of objects, her own body or self and another person, she has become a member of her culture, sharing knowledge and skills in collaboration both with and in the companionship of others.

The loneliness of the isolated child

Most young children have built memories in the safe and secure company of loving family members and specially trusted others and in doing this have been able to make a good story of their lives. Trevarthen (2005: 64) reminds us that our innate curiosity for making and sharing meaning requires what he calls

> *an exceptional emotional sensitivity that goes far beyond the expression of bodily needs. The process can build in comfort, confidence and confiding in a loving family and community or it can fall prey to fear and distress, loneliness and self-doubt. This is why infants crave the consistent sensitive company of an affectionate parent or other person who can be trusted to sustain the shared memories that have been discovered in their company.*

He later says that '*Loneliness, shame, depression and sadness are the emotions that identify loss of this collective story-making, which can be called 'socionoesis'*' (Trevarthen 2013: 206) and reminds us that socionoesis can mean making a way of life with shared meaning by story telling.

 Think about this

Edward Tronick and colleagues presented the 'still face experiment' to colleagues at the biennial meeting of the Society for Research in Child Development in 1975. Tronick et al. (1975) described a phenomenon in which an infant, after three minutes of 'interaction' with a mother who was non-responsive and expressionless initially became still and wary. Tronick then made repeated attempts to get the interaction back into its usual reciprocal pattern. When these attempts failed, what do you think the baby did? You can give your response now or go online, following this link to see for yourself: www.gottman.com/blog/the-research-the-still-face-experiment/

What is significant is that once the phenomenon had been thoroughly tested and replicated, it became a method for testing hypotheses about aspects of emotional development, communication, attachment and more. We talked of this earlier in the book but to consolidate your understanding here is another analysis of a perturbation test.

Lynne Murray and Trevarthen (1985) introduced a perturbation test designed to test the ability of infants to discriminate between reciprocal or contingent (meaning happening at the same time) and non-contingent interaction with their mothers. In this widely cited study, four infants between 6 and 12 weeks of age interacted with their mothers through a closed-circuit double television set-up. In the *Live* condition the interaction was online in real time; in the *Tape* condition the babies were presented with only a videotape of the mother. Murray and Trevarthen (1985) reported that the infants were highly interactive and content during the *Live* condition but showed distress and discomfort during the *Tape* condition.

These tests on the emotion of infants during protoconversations when the normal, and expected, reciprocal interaction is disrupted in some way have led some to suggest that any withdrawal of warmth or approval or communication has a damaging effect on the very young child. Trevarthen talks of the feelings of shame the child experiences through the actual or perceived withdrawal of love and attention by the mother or primary caregiver, which can lead the child to experience a sense of hopeless isolation. In fact Trevarthen's writing is peppered with distressing images of the isolated, enraged, withdrawn infant displaying sadness, fear and anger.

Trevarthen and Aitken (2001) suggest that the effects of maternal postnatal depression that cause the mother to display behaviours lacking pleasure, with a lowered tone of voice, flat affect and erratic timing lead to the same effects as the perturbation tests. Their conclusion is that infants may become distressed and avoidant and even develop a lasting depression that can affect communication with not only the mother, but with other persons seeking to share experience with the child.

Creating and inhabiting imaginary worlds

In this, the last chapter in the book, we turn to the young child's facility for story-telling, story-making, adopting roles, creating imaginary worlds and peopling them with imaginary creatures. Why do they engage in this so universally and with such passion? Are they finding ways to make their own real lives better or playing with and sharing the question 'What if …?'

 Think about this

We all hold a common-sense idea of what imagination is. Here are some dictionary definitions that might help us be clearer in our thinking.

- Imagination is the faculty of imagining, or of forming mental images or concepts of what is not actually present to the senses.
- It is the action or process of forming such images or concepts.
- It is the faculty of producing ideal creations consistent with reality, as in literature, as distinct from the power of creating illustrative or decorative imagery.
- A psychological definition is that imagining is the power of reproducing images stored in the memory under the suggestion of associated images (reproductive imagination) or of recombining former experiences in the creation of new images directed at a specific goal or aiding in the solution of problems (creative imagination) (dictionary.com).

There is clearly a link between memory and imagination. Trevarthen says that this is apparent in the early mother–infant interactions where the mother's action remembered by the baby becomes an elementary form of imagination to allow her to anticipate the mother's next response. You may remember reading very early in the book about the influence of brain surgeon Charles Sherrington on Trevarthen. He described the brain or nervous system as being '*the enchanted loom*' where '*millions of flashing shuttles weave a dissolving pattern, though never an abiding one*' (Sherrington 1940: 177–178).

The complexity of it all

I wrote about Hannah at the very beginning of the book and explained how my interest in babies and young children came about through observing her without being responsible for her. You may remember her passion for books, language and stories. When she was three years old and we were all living in South Africa we went on a long drive from Johannesburg to Cape Town with her parents and baby brother Ben. What happened on this journey resulted in an article I wrote in *English in Education* in 2001. It is the story of how one small child used memory, stories, books, television and what was to hand to create her own imaginary world in order to deal with her feelings.

We stopped for petrol at a garage, which was giving away a free bag of colourful plastic dinosaurs. Hannah did not get to play with them immediately because it rained and we turned on the television in our rented room. The film of *The Secret Garden* was playing and Hannah watched it from beginning to end with intent concentration. It is the story of an orphaned little girl called Mary who had been sent to live with an aunt after the death of her parents. The house in Yorkshire where she was sent was dark and gloomy but she managed to make friends with a little boy called Dickon and with her invalid cousin Colin and some animals. Nothing in the setting of the story was familiar to Hannah, living in the bright sunshine of South Africa, but she did have her rich experience of stories read and heard, told and invented, true and imagined.

The next day the sun shone and we set off to the beach, taking, of course, the dinosaurs. We all watched, entranced, as she recreated episodes from the film that spoke to her. First she selected which characters to depict, using the colours of the plastic dinosaurs to define them. In this way the pink dinosaur, for example, represented Mary. Hannah clearly understood that the pink dinosaur was not Mary but represented or stood for Mary. The pink dinosaur became a metaphor for Mary. Similarly Hannah knew that none of the plastic figures were places or people or creatures in the story. She was performing a very abstract and cognitively complex task of transforming the story into her own personal version, focusing on her interests. Her intense play ranged over several days with the colours of the 'characters' always consistent. The themes that she explored were who was good and who was bad, what was possible and what not, the potency of magic. She ignored the bad housekeeper and focused on the singing robin. Some time later she told us, 'All stories that have happy endings have a bad character.' In a sense she seemed to be trying to make sense of good and bad, right and wrong, sad and happy.

Hannah watched the film in the company of her family members and was able to turn to them for information or confirmation, to ask questions or sit on a lap when things became frightening or sad. She watched the film in the company of others. It was a sociocultural event. Later, watching other movies she began to explore narrative devices such as dream, and when I asked her if she thought the story of Peter Pan was a dream she said, 'It can't be because they would all have had to be dreaming the same thing.'

I tell this story because it reveals aspects of one very young child exploring not only reality but also fantasy and in doing so was able to represent and express her feelings and share them with others. Hannah is just one child but this is true for all young children. We come to know the world by sharing our emotions and we can share our feelings through the things we make to express them.

Trevarthen tells us that the voice may be conceived of being the first bridge between imagination and invented minds, characters in a story.

Cultural learning

Everything you have read so far must have given you an insight into just how determined the young child is to become part of her cultural world. All her physical behaviour pre-speech shows her in search of two things: an understanding of the world and a belonging to her culture. She continually engages with others, seeking to understand her world and those who inhabit it. It starts with her using movement, vision and action. Between two to four months she: is able to reach out with her hand to touch something that interests her; uses both eyes to see clearly in three dimensions; can coordinate her hand with her arm, head and eye; can use right-hand gestures as she shifts her gaze from the mother and begins to vocalise. Trevarthen records that girls do this earlier than boys. From five to eight months she begins to crawl, sit, pull herself up, stand, grasp and hold objects, look at the mother's hands, bang things together, babble and use a wide range of vocal sounds.

 Think about this

Most studies of infant social cognition have been at the level of the dyad, primarily between mother and infant. The Australian researchers, Jane Selby and Ben Bradley (2003) are critical of this approach and argue that research on dyadic mother/infant interaction or dyadic interaction between unfamiliar peers neglects the possibility that babies are born with a more general relational capacity that allows them to be socially involved with more than one person at a time. In essence they are saying that infants are biologically prepared for relationships in general, in community, rather than for forming exclusive attachments. In their research, they carried out detailed observations of babies in groups of three. Their analysis of these three-way, triadic interactions allowed them to develop a more detailed account of the role of early intersubjectivity in the development of communicative competence in a group.

Specifically they noted that the baby at six months can negotiate interests, intentions and feeling with two peers and with no adult help.

Comparable findings in pairs of infants in the middle of the first year confirm a ready sociability that is not dependent on motives of parenting.

Geraldo Fiamenghi (1997) explored the sociability of young infants not yet able to walk or talk. He based this on an experiment involving pairs of babies aged between five and nine months of age who were seated in pushchairs, opposite one another and away from their mothers. The babies showed interest in one another and used reciprocal copying of gesture, posture, facial expression, vocalisations and, interestingly, movement of feet. He regarded this as being the beginning of friendships in learning about their world.

From 9 to 18 months the young child shows great interest in the intentions and interests of others and combines her intentions with those of others. This means she is able to share tasks and meanings and ritual behaviours embedded in such things as eating with others, joining in with songs, performing to and with others and much more. As the young child becomes more used to using objects and tools and parts of her body she begins to represent her ideas and thoughts by making marks using a finger, a pen, a crayon or paint, by cutting and tearing, sticking and combining. Throughout all this time the child displays an immense interest in making and sharing meaning. A reminder here of Rogoff's work on guided participation where she noted how intently young children, involved in real-life activities with more able others, were able to join in and, by looking and listening and doing in the company of those others, became skilled and accepted into the culture.

The development of representation

Trevarthen was influenced by the work of Bruner who had long been interested in the development of representation in young children. His view was that this happens over three stages, as follows:

- First, the *enactive stage* where the infant is beginning to encode and store information. Here she plays with objects, physically exploring them. As she looks at them, shakes them, drops them, puts her tongue on them, what questions do you think she might be asking? Let us take the example of a baby shaking a rattle and hearing a noise. The baby directly manipulated the rattle and the outcome was a surprising and pleasing sound. In future, the baby may shake her hand, even if there is no rattle there, expecting her hand to produce the rattling sounds. The baby does not have an internal representation of the rattle and, therefore, does not understand that it needs the rattle in order to produce the sound.
- Second is the *iconic stage*, which is evident in children between one and six years old. This stage involves an internal representation of external objects where the child can draw on the realistic stored visual memory of something in order to represent it in some way. Take, for example, a child drawing an image of a tree. What does she have to be able to do in order

to do this? Clearly she would have to have seen a tree and retained in memory an image of it in order to be able to represent one. Here is the link made between memory and imagination.

- The third *symbolic* stage, from seven years and up, is when information is stored in the form of a code or symbol such as language. None of our babies are likely to fall onto this category.

One of the most significant thinkers on how children express their thoughts and feelings before they are able to write is Gunther Kress (1997). When a young child makes marks on a piece of paper the signs become metaphors. For the child the mark might indicate a person, an object, a place, a feeling. The marks themselves are imbued with meaning and emotion. When the young child uses an empty box to be a car or a boat, a bed or a train, the same thing happens. All of this is almost invariably set in the context of play, which you will remember is what children do voluntarily in order to make and share meaning. The child makes or does something and offers it to others to make sense of it.

Kress talks about the significance of children wanting to cut out something they have made on paper. He says that when the image comes off the page

> it enters another world. It shifts from the world of contemplation into the world of action, into the world of my practical here and now; from a world of mental action to a world of tactile, physical, objective action. While it is on the page I can do 'mental things' with it. It is a mental object, distanced from me, accessible by sight and imagination if I move into the (world of) the page. When it is off the page, I can do physical things with it. It has become a real object, accessible by feel and touch as well as by sight. It has become accessible to my imagination in a different manner and it can enter, physically, into a world of imagination constructed with other objects of whatever kind.
>
> (Kress 1997: 25–27)

The interpersonal origins of pretend play

An early protoconversation between mother and infant can be regarded as one of the precursors of expressive and representational thought. This was what Trevarthen thought and expressed in much of his work. As children encounter objects and events they assign representation and emotional values to them in the psychological 'envelope' as, for example, between mother and child. As parents play with their babies they naturally exploit the possible multimodal links among different sensory information. They point at the colour, suggest feeling the texture. They demonstrate the noise the object can make or how it can be pushed down a ramp. All of this helps the child to conceptualise objects and events using coordination, sight, sound, touch, movement. And it draws the child into possible <u>analogic</u> and <u>metaphoric</u> aspects that will play such a vital role in their developing repertoire of possibilities in pretend play. So, as the children begin to draw and paint or dance or become or pretend, they are actively involved in creating culture.

Pretend play really flourishes in the years before entering preschool or school. Children can turn objects and actions to meet their shared purposes and, in this way, can turn themselves into others. They become expert at making one thing stand for another thing, and if there are no available objects they can carry out their intentions entirely in imagination. Children can, of course, play alone, but Trevarthen argues that play motivated by pretence is creating meanings ready to be shared, and imagined as if shared. So the children become able to both exchange ideas and share the points of view of others.

Trevarthen cites the work of Jerome Kagan (1981) who, in his book *The Second Year*, stated that around the middle of the second year of life the child has a fragile social identity just as she did as an infant of between seven and eight months old. You will remember it was then that the baby's fear of strangers appeared. For the older infant this may be because the child is able to imagine behaviours in strangers that may be threatening. The second year is known as the 'terrible twos' because the ambitious, exploring toddler becomes very determined to know, and resists any question implying that she may not know, or any request to do what another wants. Rene Spitz called it the time of 'le non – the no'.

Nearly the end but not quite ...

I hope you have had the sense of Trevarthen taking us on an intriguing journey that, to quote Sylvie Rayna and Ferre Laevers, *'leaves us with a particular sense of wonder, an awareness of the richness and strengths these young persons bear in themselves'* (2014: 4). I would like to remind you that persons include babies. Rayna and Laevers are correct in claiming that Trevarthen's unique humane and scientific approach inevitably brings about a fundamental shift in our thinking and understanding of the under 3s. He insists that we take 'the perspective of the young child' as our basic premise.

And finally

Our babies in this book are on the verge of becoming part of a new culture as they enter the world of formal education. Knowing what you now know about how remarkable the human infant is in becoming an active contributor to her culture, try to ensure that her learning continues to be through her intent, active participation in things that matter to her. Let her sing and dance, speak and listen, imagine and pretend, draw and paint, think seriously and solve puzzles and always speak up for herself.

It seems fitting to end this book about babies and young children with the words of Vivian Gussin Paley in an interview for the *American Journal of Play*:

> *We must take care ... that the current academic expectations arbitrarily imposed on our children do not produce less-creative and less-happy students in our culture. It is not too late to reexamine our curriculum in the early-childhood classroom and reset the clock to an earlier time, 'when play was king and early childhood was its domain'.*

(2009: 138)

Bibliography

Ainsworth, M. D. S., Blehar, M. C. Waters, E. & Wall, S. (1978). *Patterns of Attachment: A Psychological Study of the Strange Situation*. Hillsdale, NJ: Erlbaum.

Ammaniti, M. & Ferrari, P. (2013). *Vitality Affects in Daniel Stern's Thinking – A Psychological and Neurobiological Perspective*. Infant Mental Health, 34 (5): 367–375.

Bateson, M. C. (1975). *Mother-Infant Exchanges: The Epigenesis of Conversational Interaction*. Annals of the New York Academy of Sciences, 263: 101–113.

Bateson, M. C. (1979). *'The Epigenesis of Conversational Interaction': A Personal Account of Research Development*. In Bullowa, M. (ed.), Before Speech: The Beginning of Interpersonal Communication (pp. 63–78). Cambridge: Cambridge University Press.

BBC (2016) [radio programme]. *The Life Scientific*. Frans de Waal on chimpanzees. Available at: www.bbc.co.uk/programmes/b07wt6bj

Beebe, B., Knoblauch, S., Rustin, J. & Sorter, D. (2003). *A Comparison of Meltzoff, Trevarthen, and Stern*. Psychoanalytic Dialogues, 13 (6): 809–836.

Bjørkvold, J.-R. (1991). *The Muse Within: Creativity and Communication, Song and Play from Childhood through Maturity*. New York: Harper Collins. http:// www.freidig.no/english/en_jrb.html

Bowlby, J. (1969). *Attachment and Loss* (vol. 1). New York: Basic Books. Penguin Books, reprinted in 1971.

Bråten, S. (1988). *Dialogic Mind: The Infant and the Adult in Protoconversation*. Nature, Cognition, and System, 1 (2), 187–205.

Bråten, S. (1988a). *Between Dialogical Mind and Monological Reason. Postulating the Virtual Other*. Nature, Cognition, and System I. Reidel: Kluwer Academic.

Bruner, J., Brazelton, B. & Richards, M. (1969). *Discovery of Protoconversation: The Dance of Interaction*. Center for Cognitive Studies, Harvard University (Lecture at Adlerian Society).

Bruner, J. S. (1996). *The Culture of Education*. Cambridge, MA: Harvard University Press.

Carey, S. & Xu, F. (2001). *Infants' Knowledge of Objects: Beyond Object Files and Object Tracking*, Cognition, 80 (1–2), 179–213.

Chomsky, N. (1965). *Aspects of the Theory of Syntax*. Cambridge, MA: MIT Press.

Chukovsky, K. (1963) (revised 1968). *From Two to Five*. Berkeley, CA: University of California Press.

Comenius (cited in Trevarthen 2004). *The School of Infancy. Essays on Educational Reformers* (translated by D. Bonham).

Condon, W. S. & Sander, L. W. (1974). *Synchrony Demonstrated between Movements of the Neonate and Adult Speech*. Child Development, 45 (2), 456–462.

Darwin, C. (1871, 1874). *The Descent of Man*. London: John Murray.

Darwin, C. (1877). *A Biographical Sketch of an Infant*. Mind, 2, 285–294.

Delafield-Butt, J. & Trevarthen, C. (2013). *Theories of the Development of Human Communication*. In Cobley, P. & Schultz, P. (eds), Theories and Models of Communication (pp. 199–221). Berlin/Boston: De Greyter Mouton.

Delafield-Butt, J. T. & Trevarthen, C. (2015). *The Ontogenesis of Narrative: From Moving to Meaning*. Frontiers in Psychology, 6, 11–57. doi: 10.3389/fpsyg.2015.01157

Dissanayake, E. (2000). *Art and Intimacy: How the Arts Began*. Seattle and London: University of Washington Press.

Donaldson, M. (1978). *Children's Minds*. London: Harper Collins.

Donaldson, M. (1992). *Human Minds*. London: Allen Lane/Penguin Books.

Dunn, J. & Kenrick, C. (1982). *Siblings: Love, Envy and Understanding*. Cambridge, MA: Harvard University Press.

Dunn, M. (1988). *The Beginnings of Social Understanding*. Oxford: Blackwell.

educationscotland (2016). Pre-Birth to Three: Professor Colwyn Trevarthen – Relationships. Available at: https://www.youtube.com/watch?v=pW42_wYNGWk

Engel, J., Timothy, A., Pedley, T., Aicardi, J., Dichter, M., Moshé, S., Perucca, E. & Trimble, M. (2007). *Epilepsy: A Comprehensive Textbook*. Lippincott: William and Wilkins.

Fiamenghi, J. L. (1997) *Emotional Expression in Infants' Interactions with Their Mirror Images: An Exploratory Study*. Journal of Reproductive and Infant Psychology, 25 (2), 152–160.

Galanaki, E. (n.d.). *Loneliness and Solitude in Trevarthen's Work: Some Notes and Questions*. (Publication details removed from the Internet.)

Gentilucci, M. & Corballis, M. (2006). *From Manual Gesture to Speech: A Gradual Transition*. Neuroscience and Biobehavioural Review, 30, 949–960.

Goldin-Meadow, S. (2005). *The Resilience of Language: What Gesture Creation in Deaf Children Can Tell Us about How All Children Learn Language*. Hove and New York: Psychology Press.

Goldin-Meadow, S. (2009). *How Gesture Promotes Learning throughout Childhood*. Child Development Perspectives, 3, 106–111.

Gratier, M. (2003). *The Benefits of Talking with a Psychologist: A Mother's Narrative*. In Enfances e Psy No 1 Parents and Professional. Eres.

Gratier, M. & Devouche, E. (2011). *Imitation and Repetition of Prosodie Contour in Vocal Interaction at 3 Months*. Developmental Psychology, 47 (1), 67.

Gratier, M. & Trevarthen, C. (2007). *Voice, Vitality and Meaning: On the Shaping of the Infant's Utterances in Willing Engagement with Culture. Comment on Bertau's 'On the Notion of Voice'*. International Journal for Dialogical Science, 2(1), Special Issue: Developmental Origins of the Dialogical Self, M. Bertau & M. Goncalves, Guest Editors, 169–181.

Gratier, M. & Trevarthen, C. (2008). *Musical Narrative and Motives for Culture in Mother-Infant Vocal Interaction*. The Journal of Consciousness Studies, 15, 122–158.

Gray, P. (2012). *The Value of a Play-Filled Childhood in Development of the Hunter-Gatherer Individual*. In D. Narváez (ed.), Evolution, Early Experience and Human Development: From Research to Practice and Policy (pp. 352–370). Oxford and New York: Oxford University Press.

Habermas, J. (1970). *Towards a Theory of Communicative Competence*. Inquiry: Interdisciplinary Journal of Philosophy, 13, 1–4.

Halliday, M. (1975). *Learning How to Mean: Explorations in the Development of Language*. London: Edward Arnold.

Halliday, M. (1993). *Towards a Language-based Theory of Learning*. Linguistics and Education, 5, 93–116.

Handal, A., Lozoff, B., Breilh, J. & Harlow, S. D. (2007). *Neurobehavioral Development in Children with Potential Exposure to Pesticides*. Epidemiology, 18 (3), 312–320.

Hubley, P. & Trevarthen, C. (1979). *Sharing a Task in Infancy*. In I. Uzgiris (ed.), Social Interaction During Infancy, New Directions for Child Development, 4, (pp. 57–80). San Francisco, CA: Jossey-Bass.

Huizinga, J. (1955) Homo Ludens: *A Study of the Play-Element in Culture*. London, Boston and Henley: Routledge and Kegan Paul.

Jahoda, G. & Lewis, I. M. (1988 first edition). *Acquiring Culture: Cross-cultural Studies in Child Development*. London and New York: Psychology Press.

Kagan, J. (1981). *The Second Year: The Emergence of Self-Awareness*. Cambridge, MA: Harvard University Press.

Kiernan. K. E. & Mensah, A. H. (2009). *Poverty, Maternal Depression, Family Status and Children's Cognitive and Behavioural Development in Early Childhood: A Longitudinal Study*. Journal of Social Policy, 38 (4), 569–588.

Kokkinaki, T. & Vitalaki, E. (2013). *Comparing Spontaneous Imitation in Grandmother-Infant Interaction: A Three Generation Familial Study*. The International Journal of Ageing and Human Development, 9 (2), 259–275.

Kress, G. (1997). *Before Writing: Rethinking the Paths to Literacy*. London and New York: Routledge.

Malaguzzi, L. (2007). *The Hundred Languages of Children*. Reggio Children. Travelling exhibition.

Malloch, S. (1999). *Mothers and Infants and Communicative Musicality*. Musicae Scientiae, 3, 29–57.

Malloch, S. & Trevarthen, C. (2000). *The Dance of Wellbeing: Defining the Musical Therapeutic Effect*. Norwegian Journal of Music Therapy, 9 (2), 3–17.

Malloch, S. & Trevarthen, C. (2009). *Communicative Musicality: Exploring the Basis of Human Companionship*. Oxford: Oxford University Press.

Malloch, S., Sharp, D., Campbell, D. M., Campbell, A. M. & Trevarthen, C. (1997). *Measuring the Human Voice: Analysing Pitch, Timing, Loudness and Voice Quality in Mother/Infant Communication*. Proceedings of the Institute of Acoustics, 19 (5), 495–500.

Matthews, J. (1994). *Helping Children to Draw and Paint in Early Childhood: Children and Visual Representation*. London and New York: Hodder & Stoughton.

Maturana, H. R. & Varela, F. J. (1972/1980). *Autopoiesis and Cognition: The Realization of the Living*. Dordrecht, Holland: D. Reidel Publishing Company.

Meltzoff, A. & Brooks, R. (2007). *Intersubjectivity before Language in Three Windows in Perverbal Sharing*. In Bråten, S. (ed.), On Being Moved: From Mirror Neurons to Empathy (pp. 149–174). Philadelphia, PA: John Benjamins.

Murray, L. (1999). *The Role of Infant Factors in Maternal Depression*. Infant Observation, 3 (1), 63–73.

Murray, L. (2014). *The Psychology of Babies: How Relationships Support Development from Birth to Two*. London: Constable and Robinson.

Murray, L. & Trevarthen, C. (1985). *Emotional Regulation of Interactions Between Two-Month-Olds and Their Mother.* In Field, T. & Fox, N. (eds), Social Perception in Infants (pp. 177–197). Norwood, NJ: Ablex.

Murray, L. & Trevarthen, C. (1986). *The Infant's Role in Mother-Infant Communication.* Journal of Child Language, 13, 15–29.

Murray, L., Cooper, P., Creswell, C., Schofield, E. & Sack, C. (2007). *The Effects of Material Social Phobia on Mother-Infant Interactions and Infant Social Responsiveness.* Journal of Child Psychology and Psychiatry, 48 (1), 45–52.

Nagy, E. & Molnar, P. (2004). *Homo imitans or homo provocans? Human Imprinting Model of Neonatal Imitation.* Infant Behaviour and Development, V1, 54–63.

Nagy, E. & Trevarthen, C. (2011). *What Is It Like to Be a Person Who Knows Nothing? Defining the Active Intersubjective Mind of a Newborn Human Being.* Infant and Child Development, 20 (1), 119–135. Special edition edited by Nagy.

Narváez, D. (2012) (ed.). *Evolution, Early Experience and Human Development: From Research to Practice and Policy* (pp. 352–370). Oxford and New York: Oxford University Press.

National Scientific Council on the Developing Child (2007). *The Science of Early Childhood Development: Closing the Gap Between What We Know and What We Do.* www.developingchild.net

Nelson, C. (2000). *Neural Plasticity and Human Development: The Role of Early Experience in Sculpting Memory Systems.* Developmental Sciences, 3 (3), 115–136.

Oxford Dictionaries (2010). Intersubjective. Oxford: Oxford University Press.

Paley, V. G. (1981). *Wally's Stories: Conversations in the Kindergarten.* Cambridge, MA: Harvard University Press.

Paley, V. G. (1988). *Bad Guys Don't Have Birthdays: Fantasy Play at Four.* Chicago: University of Chicago Press.

Paley, V. G. (2009). *The Importance of Fantasy, Fairness and Friendship in Children's Play: An Interview With Vivian Gussin Paley.* American Journal of Play, 2 (2). Available at: www.journalofplay.org/sites/www.journalofplay.org/files/pdf-articles/2-2-interview-paley-fantasy-fairness-friendship.pdf

Panksepp, J. & Northoff, G. (2009). *The Trans-Species Core Self: The Emergence of Active, Cultural and Neuro-Ecological Agents Through Self-Related Processing Within Subcortical Midline Networks.* Consciousness and Cognition, 18, 193–215.

Pascoe, M, Bissessur, D. & Mayers, P. (2016). *Mothers' Perceptions of Their Premature Infant's Communication: A Description of Two Cases.* Health SA Gesondheid, 21, 143–154.

Piontelli, S. ([1992]2010). *From Fetus to Child: An Observational and Psychoanalytical Study.* London: Routledge.

Porges, S. W. (2011). *The Polyvagal Theory: Neurophysiological Foundations of Emotions, Attachment, Communication and Self-Regulation.* New York: W.W. Norton & Company.

Powers, N. & Trevarthen, C. (2009). *Voices of Shared Emotion and Meaning: Young Infants and Their Mothers in Scotland and Japan.* In Malloch, S. & Trevarthen, C. (eds), Communicative Musicality: Exploring the Basis of Human Companionship (pp. 209–240). Oxford: Oxford University Press.

Psychobabble (2012). Embodied Psychotherapies: Interview with Prof. Trevarthen. The University of Edinburgh. Issue 4, November. Available at: www.think.psy.ed.ac.uk/wp-content/uploads/2015/11/Psychobabble_issue4.pdf

Psychology Dictionary (2017). Co-operative motive. Available at: http://psychologydictionary.org/cooperative-motive/

Rayna, S. & Laevers, F. (eds) (2014). *Understanding the Under 3s and the Implications for Education*. Abingdon and New York: Routledge.

Reddy, V. (2003). *On Being the Object of Attention: Implications for Self-Other Consciousness*. Trends in Cognitive Science, 7 (9), 397–402.

Reddy, V. (2008). *How Infants Know Minds*. Cambridge, MA: Harvard University Press.

Reddy, V. & Trevarthen, C. (2004). *What We Learn About Babies from Engaging With Their Emotions*, Zero to Three, 24 (3), 9–15.

Reissland, N. (2012). *The Development of Emotional Intelligence*. London and New York: Routledge.

Reissland, N. & Kisilevsky, B. (2016). *Fetal Development*. New York: Springer.

Richards, M. (1980). *World of the Newborn*. New York: Harper & Row.

Rochat, R., Passos-Ferreira, C. & Salem, P. (2009). *Three Levels of Intersubjectivity in Early Development*. In Carassa, A., Morganti, F. & Riva, G. (eds), Enacting Intersubjectivity: Paving the Way for a Dialogue Between Cognitive Science, Social Cognition and Neuroscience (pp. 173–190). Lugano, Switzerland: Università della Svizzera Italiana.

Rogoff, B. (1990). *Apprentice in Thinking: Cognitive Development in Social Context*. Oxford: Oxford University Press.

Rogoff, B., Paradise, R., Meiia Arauz, R., Correa-Chavez, M. & Angelillo, C. (2003). *First Hand Learning Through Intent Participation*. Annual Review of Psychology, 54, 175–203.

Ryan, J. (1974). *Early Language Development: Towards a Communicative Analysi*s. In Richards, M. P. M. (ed.), The Integration of the Child into the Social World (pp. 185–213). Cambridge: Cambridge University Press.

Sacks, O. (2007, first edition). *Musicophilia: Tales of Music and the Brain*. New York: Random House.

Selby, J. & Bradley, B. (2003). *Observing Infants in Groups: The Clan Revisited*. Infant Observation, 7 (2–3), 107–122.

Sherrington, C. S. (1940 revised 1953) *Man on His Nature*. Cambridge: Cambridge University Press.

Sherry, K. & Draper, C. (2013). *The Relationship Between Gross Motor Skills and School Readiness in Early Childhood: Making the Case in South Africa*. Early Childhood and Care, 183 (9), 1293–1310.

Shore, A. (1997). *Attachment and the Regulation of the Right Brain*. Attachment and Human Development, 2 (1), 23–47.

Sightlines Initiative (n.d.). Born for Art, and the Joyful Companionship of Fiction, Colwyn Trevarthen, Department of Psychology, University of Edinburgh. www.sightlines-initiative.com

Smidt, S. (2001). *All Stories that Have a Happy Ending Have a Bad Character: A Young Child Responds to Televisual Texts*. English in Education, 35 (2), 25–33.

Smidt, S. (2009). *Introducing Vygotsky: A Guide for Practitioners and Students in Early Years Education*. Abingdon: Routledge.

Smidt, S. (2011). *Introducing Bruner: A Guide for Practitioners and Students in Early Years Education*. Abingdon: Routledge.

Steele, R. & Threadgold, T. (1987). *Language Topics*. London and New York: Routledge.

Stensaeth, K. & Trondalen, G. (2012). *Dialogue on Intersubjectivity: An Interview with Stein Braten and Colwyn Trevarthen*. Voices: A World Forum for Music Therapy, 12 (3), 1–27.

Stephen, C., Dunlop, A., Trevarthen, C. & Marwick, H. (2003). *Meeting the Needs of Children from Birth to Three: Research Evidence and Implications for Out-of-Home Provision.* Scottish Executive: Education Department, Insight, 6. Available at: www.gov.scot/Publications/2003/06/17458/22696

Stern, D. (1977 reprint 2002) *The First Relationship: Infant and Mother.* Cambridge, MA: Harvard University Press.

Stern, D. ([1985]1993, and reprinted many times). *The Interpersonal World of the Infant: A View from Psychoanalysis and Developmental Psychology.* New York: Karnac.

Stern, D. (1993). *L'enveloppe prénarrative.* Journal de la Psychanalyse de l'enfant, 14, 13–65.

Stern, D. (2001). *Face-to-Face Play.* In Jaffe, J., Beebe, B., Feldstein, S., Crown, C. & Jasnow, M. D. (eds), Rhythms of Dialogue in Infancy: Coordinated Timing in Development. Monographs of the Society for Research in Child Development, 66.

Stern, D., Jaffe, J., Beebe, B., & Bennett, S. (1975). *Vocalizing in Unison and in Alternation. T Modes of Communication within the Mother-Infant Dyad.* Annals of the New York Academy of Sciences, 263, 89–100. Reprinted in L. Bloom (ed.), Readings in Language Development (pp. 115–127). New York: Wiley, 1978.

Stern, D. N. (1995). *The Motherhood Constellation: A Unified View of Parent–Infant Psychotherapy.* New York, NY: Basic Books.

Stern, D. N. (2010). *Forms of Vitality: Exploring Dynamic Experience in Psychology, the Arts, Psychotherapy and Development.* Oxford and New York: Oxford University Press.

Tallis, R. (2011). *Michaelangelo's Finger: An Exploration of Everyday Transcendence.* London: Atlantic Books.

Tomlinson, M. & Walker, R. (2010). *Recurrent Poverty: The Impact of Family and Labour Market Changes.* York: Joseph Rowntree Foundation.

Trevarthen, C. (1988). *Universal Cooperative Motives: How Infants Begin to Know the Language, Skills and Culture of Their Parents.* In Jahoda, G. & Lewis, I. (eds), Acquiring Culture: Cross Cultural Studies in Child Development (pp. 37–90). Beckenham: Croom Helm.

Trevarthen, C. (1990). *Signs Before Speech.* In Sebeok, T. & Umiker-Sebeok, J. (eds), The Semiotic Web (pp. 689–755). New York and Amsterdam: Mouton de Gruyter.

Trevarthen, C. (1993). *The Self Born in Intersubjectivity: The Psychology of an Infant Communicating.* In Neisser, U. (ed.), The Perceived Self: Ecological and Interpersonal Sources of Self Knowledge (pp. 121–173). New York: Cambridge University.

Trevarthen, C. (1993a). *The Function of Emotions in Early Infant Communication and Development.* In Nadel, J. & Camaioni, L. (eds), New Perspectives in Early Communicative Development (pp. 48–81). London: Routledge.

Trevarthen, C. (1998). *The Child's Need to Learn a Culture.* In Woodhead, M., Faulkner, D. & Littleton, K. (eds), Cultural Worlds of Early Childhood (pp. 87–100). New York: Routledge.

Trevarthen, C. (1998a). *The Concept and Foundations of Infant Intersubjectivity.* In Bråten, S. (ed.), Intersubjective Communication and Emotion in Early Ontogeny (pp. 15–46). Cambridge: Cambridge University Press.

Trevarthen, C. (2001). *The Neurobiology of Early Communication: Intersubjective Regulations in Human Brain Development.* In Kalverboer A. F. & Gramsbergen, A. (eds), Handbook on Brain and Behaviour in Human Development (pp. 841–882). Dordrecht, The Netherlands: Kluwer.

Trevarthen, C. (2001a). *Intrinsic Motives for Companionship in Understanding: The Origin, Development and Significance for Infant Mental Health.* Infant Mental Health Journal, 22 (1–2), 95–131.

Trevarthen, C. (2002). *Making Sense of Infants Making Sense*. Intellica 2002/1, 34, 161–188.

Trevarthen, C. (2004). *Learning About Ourselves, From Children: Why a Growing Human Brain Needs Interesting Companions*. Research and Clinical Centre for Child Development, Annual Report 2002–2003, 26, 9–44. Graduate School of Education, Hokkaido University.

Trevarthen, C. (2005). *Stepping Away from the Mirror: Pride and Shame in Adventures of Companionship. Reflections on the Nature and Emotional Needs of Infant Intersubjectivity*. In Carter, C. S., Ahnert, L., Grossman, K. E., Hardy, S. B., Lamb, M. E., Porges, S. W. & Sachser, N. (eds), Attachment and Bonding: A New Synthesis. Dahlem Workshop Report 92 (pp. 55–84). Cambridge, MA: The MIT Press.

Trevarthen, C. (2008). *The Value of Creative Art in Childhood*. Children in Europe, 14, 6–9.

Trevarthen, C. (2009a). *Why Attachment Matters in Sharing Meaning*. SAIA Seminar in Glasgow.

Trevarthen, C. (2009b). *The Intersubjective Psychobiology of Human Meaning: Learning of Culture Depends on Interest for Co-Operative Practical Work and Affection for the Joyful Art of Good Company*. Psychoanalytic Dialogues, 19 (5), 507–518.

Trevarthen, C. (2010). *What Is It Like To Be a Person Who Knows Nothing? Defining the Active Intersubjective Mind of a Newborn Human Being*. Infant and Child Development, 20 (1), 119–135. Special edition edited by Nagy.

Trevarthen, C. (2011). *What Young Children Give to Their Learning, Making Education Work to Sustain a Community and Its Culture*. European Childhood Education Research Journal 19 (2), Special Issue: Birth to Three, S. Rayna & F. Laevers, 173–193.

Trevarthen, C. (2013). *Born for Art, and the Joyful Companionship of Fiction*. In Narvaez, D., Panksepp, J., Schore, A. & Gleason, T. (eds), Evolution, Early Experience and Human Development: From Research to Practice and Policy (pp. 202–218). New York: Oxford University Press.

Trevarthen, C. (2013a). *What Young Children Know About Living and Learning With Companions*. Nordisk Barnehageforskning, 6 (25), 1–9.

Trevarthen, C. (2013b). *Artful Learning Makes Sense*. Early Education, British Association for Early Childhood Education, 90th Anniversary of Early Education. Article 1.

Trevarthen, C. (2013c). Obituary: *Remembering Daniel Stern*. Body, Movement and Dance in Psychotherapy, 8 (1), 64–65.

Trevarthen, C. (2015). *Awareness of Infants: What Do They, and We, Seek?* Psychoanalytic Enquiry 35 (4), 395–416.

Trevarthen, C. & Aitken, K. J. (1994). *Brain Development, Infant Communication, and Empathy Disorders: Intrinsic Factors in Child Mental Health*. Development and Psychopathology, 6 (4), 597–633.

Trevarthen, C. & Aitken, K. J. (2001). *Infant Intersubjectivity: Research, Theory and Clinical Applications*. Annual Research Review. The Journal of Child Psychology and Psychiatry and Allied Disciplines, 42 (1), 3–48.

Trevarthen, C. & Aitken, K. J. (2003). *Regulation of Brain Development and Age-Related Changes in Infants' Motives: The Developmental Function of 'Regressive Periods'*. In Heimann, M., Regression Periods in Human Infancy (pp. 107–184). Mahwah, NJ: Erlbaum.

Trevarthen, C. & Burford, B. (1995). *The Central Role of Parents: How They Can Give Power to a Motor Impaired Child's Acting Experiencing and Sharing*. European Journal of Special Needs Education, 10 (2), 138–148.

Trevarthen, C., & Delafield-Butt, J. (2013). *Biology of Shared Experience and Language Development: Regulations for the Intersubjective Life of Narratives.* In Legerstee, M., Haley, D. W. & Bornstein, M. H. (eds), The Infant Mind: Origins of the Social Brain. New York: Guilford Press.

Trevarthen, C. & Delafield-Butt, J. (2015). *The Infant's Creative Vitality, in Projects of Self-Discovery and Shared Meaning: How They Anticipate School and Make It Fruitful.* In Robson, S. & Quinn, S. F. (eds), The Routledge International Handbook of Young Children's Thinking and Understanding (pp. 3–18). London and New York: Routledge.

Trevarthen, C. & Hubley, P. (1978). *Secondary Intersubjectivity: Confidence, Confiding and Acts of Meaning in the First Year.* In Lock, A. (ed.), Action, Gesture and Symbol (pp. 183–229). London: Academic Press.

Trevarthen, C. & Malloch, S. (2002). *Musicality and Music Before Three: Human Vitality and Invention Shared with Pride.* Zero to Three, 23 (2), 10–18.

Trevarthen, C. & Reddy, V. (2007). *Consciousness in Infants.* In Velman, M. & Schneider, S. (eds), A Companion to Consciousness (pp. 41–57). Oxford: Blackwell.

Trevarthen, C., Aitken, K., Papoudi, D. & Robarts, J. (1993). *Children with Autism: Diagnosis, Prevalence in Scotland and Interventions to Meet Their Needs.* Edinburgh: Scottish Education Department.

Tronick, E., Als, H. & Brazelton, T. B. (1980). *Monadic Phases: A Structural Descriptive Analysis of Infant–Mother Face-to-Face Interaction.* Merrill-Palmer Quarterly of Behavior and Development, 26, 3–24.

Tronick, E., Adamson, L. B., Als, H. & Brazelton, T. B. (1975, April). Infant Emotions in Normal and Pertubated Interactions. Paper presented at the biennial meeting of the Society for Research in Child Development, Denver, CO.

Turner, M. (1996). *The Literary Mind: The Origins of Thought and Language.* New York and Oxford: Oxford University Press.

Tzourio-Mazoyer, N., Landeau, B., Papathanassio, D., Crivello, F., Etard, N., Delcroix, B., Mazoyer, T. & Jolio, M. (2002). *Automated Anatomical Labelling in SPM Using Anatomical Parcellation of the MNI MRI Single-Subject Brain.* NeuroImage, 15, 273–289.

Van Puyvelde, M., Vanfleteren, P., Loots, G., Deschuyffeleer, S., Vinck, B., Jacquet, W. & Verhelst, W. (2010). *Tonal Synchrony in Mother-Infant Interaction Based on Harmonic and Pentatonic Series.* Infant Behavioural Development, 33 (4), 387–400.

Vygotsky, L. (1978). *Mind in Society.* Cambridge, MA: Harvard University Press.

Index